the ride

the ride

CYCLING FOR LIFE

William G. Gisel Jr.

Foreword by
MIKE FRAYSSE,
founder of
AMERICA'S CYCLING TEAM

Prometheus Books
59 John Glenn Drive
Amherst, New York 14228-2197

Published 2005 by Prometheus Books

Inquiries should be addressed to
Prometheus Books
59 John Glenn Drive
Amherst, New York 14228–2197
VOICE: 716–691–0133, ext. 207
FAX: 716–564–2711
WWW.PROMETHEUSBOOKS.COM

09 08 07 06 05   5 4 3 2 1

Library of Congress Cataloging-in-Publication Data

Gisel, William G.
      The ride : cycling for life / William G. Gisel, Jr.; foreword by Mike Fraysse.
          p. cm.
      ISBN 1–59102–276–2 (pbk.: alk. paper)
      1. Bicycle touring—Social aspects—Alaska. 2. Alaska AIDS Vaccine Ride (2001)—Personal
narratives. 3. Gisel, William G. I. Title.

GV1045.5.A4G57 2005
796.6'4'09798—dc22
                                                                                2004026872

Printed in the United States of America on acid-free paper

To

my life partner, Mary,

and my lifelong friend Ted,

both who urged me to "just do it"

and who, in their own ways,

rode with me all the way

—and—

to my mother, Katherine Gisel,

who succumbed to cancer just two days ago.

With her grace and indomitable spirit,

she inspired my every step and my every pedal.

My proceeds from this book will benefit

Roswell Park Cancer Institute,

where she and so many others

receive extraordinary care.

Contents

Foreword

Some might say I have a bicycling birthright. My grandfather, Emile, was an Olympic manager and coach for the 1928 and 1932 games. My father, Victor, was an international manager and coach for more than three decades. I myself was an Olympic coach and manager for the 1976 and 1984 games. During my career, I've had the honor of preparing some of the world's best cyclists for their Olympic and World Championship goals.

It is not often that I come across a rider who stands out like Bill Gisel.

When Bill decided to make his historic ride, he sought advice and he followed it. Many people would have attempted this five-hundred-mile ride on emotion alone and would not have understood the level of planning and foresight required to succeed.

Bill did not simply hop on a bike and blindly begin his trek across Alaska.

He did his homework: He researched the best bicycle for his trip; he studied how to maintain it; he learned how to train for long-distance rides. Bill prepared both his physical and mental being so that he could attain his goal of not only embarking on the grueling five-hundred-mile ride but finishing it well.

Bill learned early on that this event was going to be more than just the ride. It was going to be about all it took to go on the journey of a lifetime. I like the quote from Bill's friend Bushy: "It's not about destination, it's about the trip." Sometimes we get so focused on our goal that we don't enjoy the experiences along the way. Not Bill.

Discovering how much he was truly undertaking and realizing the family and work obligations that he was sacrificing could have been daunting. But Bill did not make excuses—he made a plan. He buckled down like a true competitor and got busy.

Despite the obvious physical repercussions that go along with intense training, he also witnessed bad crashes and narrowly avoided machines, beasts, and road hazards. Bill persevered. He never lost sight of his goal: to help a cause in which he believes and to feel the self-satisfaction and pride that come along with achieving a remarkable accomplishment.

I have had the honor to coach two of the world's greatest cyclists: Lance Armstrong and Greg LeMond. They overcame tremendous odds—cancer, a near-fatal gunshot wound—yet never complained and never doubted they could achieve their goals. In Bill, I see these same traits. Bill Gisel not only took his vision and rode with it but also did it like a true champion.

MIKE FRAYSSE
Member of the Bicycle Hall of Fame
Olympic Manager and Coach

The Challenge

1

Sundays

I hate phone calls on Sunday nights at home. Sundays are sacred, and not just in religious terms. Mary and I have always preferred to be home on Sunday evenings so we can soak up those last few hours of the weekend with our children, Hanna and Will, before the start of yet another too-busy week. Invitations to Buffalo Sabres hockey games, concerts, charity dinners, and myriad other social opportunities are routinely rejected because they violate the "not-on-Sunday" rule. Perhaps that's why the invitations have slowed in recent years. But no matter, because we wouldn't have it any other way.

So when the phone rang one Sunday evening late in March 2001, I was mildly perturbed. Once we've successfully protected a Sunday evening, even phone calls are an unwelcome intrusion. When Hanna announced that it was Ted on the phone, I lightened up a little. Lifelong best friends do deserve some deference even in the face of the "not-on-Sunday" rule. As I rose from the couch, I had no premonition of how influential this conversation would be. I assumed Ted was calling about an insurance form I'd failed to sign (he's also my insurance agent) or perhaps to propose a get-together during our upcoming family trip to Florida.

Ted's first words were "Gies, I've got another adventure for you!" This intro alone piqued my interest because for Ted, seeking adventure is a way of life. Fortunately for me, many of the first twenty-four years of my life were punctuated with memorable co-adventures with Ted. Although our ages and locales ranged from eight-year-olds camping on a Lake Erie beach to twenty-two-year-olds running with the bulls in Spain, a thread of consistency linked all these forays together. That link was in large part the spontaneity of each venture.

While there were certainly a few harrowing moments along the way, we were not mindless risk takers. Our spontaneity was spawned not by recklessness but rather by Ted's insatiable curiosity. Part tourist, part student, and part thrill seeker, Ted lives life large, and I was lucky enough to be his sidekick in what friends and family used to refer to as "Bill and Ted's Great Adventure."

Predictably, the past twenty years have brought fewer "Bill and Ted" adventures, as spontaneity and naiveté have given way to the responsibility and maturity that come with families and careers. Yes, we managed to institutionalize an annual western ski trip with a collection of college friends. But even as we challenge each other to ever steeper terrains, these ski trips are as much about reliving long-past college days as they are about creating new adventures.

When Ted proposed a potential new adventure, I had no doubt it would be unique. His voice sparking with excitement, Ted launched into his sales pitch for the 2001 AIDS Vaccine Ride, a five-hundred-mile bike trip from Fairbanks to Anchorage, Alaska, to raise funds for AIDS

Ted is also Hanna's godfather.

Part tourist, part student, and part thrill seeker, Ted lives life large, and I was lucky enough to be his sidekick in what friends and family used to refer to as "Bill and Ted's Great Adventure."

vaccine research. I'm sure he expected a polite rejection based on those ready-made twin excuses of "too little time" and "too much to do." Undaunted, he rattled through his pitch and insisted that I check out the Web site for the ride. I told him I'd get back to him in a day or two.

When I hung up the phone, Mary looked up from her position in front of the stove and asked, "What was that about?" She could tell from my end of the conversation that it was not a routine Ted call.

As I gave her the details, my tone of voice already signaled my probable rejection of Ted's offer. It would be so much easier to beg off.

Mary's reaction was simple and straight. Before I could roll out my standard rationalizations, she said casually, "You should do it," as she stirred the pot in front of her.

Maybe it was the simple clarity of her declaration or the fact that I was coming off a stressful couple weeks at work. Perhaps it was the looming shadow of my fiftieth birthday, just twenty months away. Some combination of unknown forces carried me without reason from "no way" to "yes" in a mere moment. I didn't need to carefully weigh the pros and cons, the reasons for and against. The decision was made; the weight lifted from my mind, my pulse quickened.

The due diligence review of the Web site became a formality. I was joining Ted to ride five hundred miles through Alaska in just six days in August.

Palm Island

Ten days after Ted's call, Mary, Hanna, Will, and I were enjoying an April week at Palm Island on the west coast of Florida, our seventh straight year visiting this laid-back barrier island during the kids' spring break. It took me a few years to get the hang of the place. In the early years, I felt driven to spearhead endless new activities and experiences for the family. Whether it be fishing, boating, nature tours, or volleyball games, we were going to leverage every minute of our vacation time.

After years of sustained passive resistance from the rest of the family, I realized that the absence of coordinated activities and generated experiences was exactly the point of this place. I've learned to appreciate that the biggest decisions of the day are "beach or pool"—and "Cheerios or Frosted Flakes." While I still admittedly have brief pangs of lost opportunity as I count the days remaining in our vacation, I have become content to let the days melt away with no discernible accomplishments.

My thoughts and even my dreams have followed a similar course on each of our Palm Island vacations. For at least three days, my waking and even my nonwaking thoughts are consumed by my work as chief operating officer of Rich Products Corporation. Rich is a privately owned frozen-food processor with a broad product portfolio that ranges from desserts, to bakery items, to shrimp entrees. With sales of $2 billion spread across more than fifty countries, it is a dynamic, fast-paced business. It's not possible to close a mental door on work thoughts, especially given the dubious advancements of e-mail, voice mail, and other technological intrusions into the white spaces of

Mary, Hanna, Will, and me in Palm Island in 2000.

our lives. I always bring a good book to read to help ward off these real-world ponderings.

After a few days, I find that the theme of the book captures at least a portion of my thoughts. This time it was Jeff Shaara's *Of Gods and Generals*, part of a father/son trilogy about the Civil War. As I read about the grueling hardships endured by the soldiers on both sides of the "war between the states," my worries about the hardships that Ted and I would encounter on our Alaska ride seemed petty and self-indulgent. Yet I was starting to consciously size up the challenge. No one was around to reassure me that a forty-eight-year-old, office-bound, type-A businessman had the physical or mental strength to take this on. I would need to convince myself.

After years of sustained

passive resistance from the

rest of the family,

I realized that the absence

of coordinated activities

and generated experiences

was exactly the point

of this place.

Bar Exam II

Already four weeks had passed since I committed to join Ted on the AIDS ride. That meant four fewer weeks to get in shape and to learn the "ins and outs" of long-distance road biking. Had I taken the time up front to learn more about this challenge, I would not have been so quick to commit. My initial impressions and expectations at the outset included "This will be very pleasant—join a group of fellow bicyclers for a picturesque late summer tour of Alaska. Yes, it's a long way, but I'm in pretty good shape, so it shouldn't be too tough to get ready." As I moved up the learning curve on this pedaling experience, my more informed impressions evolved to "Oh, my God, what am I doing to myself?!"

In the spring of 1978, I had spent two months cramming for the New York State bar exam, which occupied my every waking thought for the full eight weeks. The size and scope of the test intimidated even the brightest law students. During those pre-exam weeks, other parts of my life gave way because I knew with certainty that I could never be fully ready. It was patently impossible to memorize every nuance of every subject of New York State law. I had to believe that if I studied relentlessly, I would arrive adequately prepared, even though I also knew that one out of three applicants would fail. Confidence was my enemy during those weeks. I needed the motivations of fear and self-doubt to keep me poring over my notes and outlines every available minute of every hour of every day.

Exactly one week after signing up for the ride, I received a packet of information covering a variety of subjects, from fund-raising techniques to travel logistics. As

I accumulated an abundance of materials to learn more about bicycling.

my eyes descended the index of the thickest booklet, my attention was immediately drawn to the sections on training and health. The training section led off with a stark admission on my behalf: "You are not currently in good enough shape to complete this ride." It then detailed a highly recommended six-month training program that would assure my buildup of the needed strength and endurance. I paused at the end of this section and looked up, counting in my head the number of months before the start of the ride. The rest of May, June, July, plus two weeks in August . . . less than three-and-a-half months' time to train, and I still didn't own a road bike.

While the Alaska ride lacked the life-shaping gravity of the bar exam, it felt the same. Still three months away, it dominated my thoughts and my scarce idle time away from work. The more I learned about the experience, the greater my self-doubt and fear. I wrapped my mind around this fear and put it to use. As with the bar exam, those dark emotions became essential motivators to take on the bearish training regimen for this test. I realized that I would not arrive in Alaska fully prepared. The new question was "Can I learn and train enough to get there adequately prepared?"

Reading on, my dismay deepened as I scanned the details of the recommended training. I concluded it must have been designed by some bicycle junkie who, based on the suggested number of hours on the bike each week, could not possibly have had a family or any career other than as a bike messenger.

My fear needle took a considerable jump, but I still needed a better benchmark for my current state of readiness. I needed to experience first-hand how far I had to go to get into shape. I needed to do a test ride.

While the Alaska ride lacked the life-shaping gravity of the bar exam, it felt the same.

17

Discovering the Bicycle World

Test Ride

I conducted my test ride in mid-May in Niagara County on my Fuji hybrid bike. A couple days earlier, I had been talking about my upcoming ride to a coworker who, in the spirit of conversation, asked me what kind of bike I owned.

"Well, it's red, and I think it cost about eighty bucks when I bought it fifteen or sixteen years ago." Consistent with my status as an occasional "take-a-ride-for-a-change-of-pace-in-my-exercise-routine" biker, my bicycle was a modest, all-purpose, ride-around-the-neighborhood type. Certainly it would serve the purpose of my test ride.

I started in the town of Wheatfield, not far from Niagara Falls, at nine o'clock on a cool but sunny Saturday morning. My carefully mapped triangular route took me north to Lake Ontario; west to the Town of Lewiston, on the Niagara River below the Falls; and then back on a southeastern track to my starting point. Total distance was about forty-five miles, about half of what I would have to cover each of my six days in Alaska.

I learned three lessons on my test ride. First, a headwind, even a light one, has a very depressing effect on progress. Second, even with brief rest stops, I averaged a meager nine miles per hour, which is considerably less than the twelve-miles-per-hour minimum needed to complete Alaska. Third, I needed a new bike.

The ride was pretty flat, except for the final twenty minutes, which took me back up the steep Niagara escarpment. The escarpment is a ridge that runs east to west across Niagara County to the river and continues west into Ontario, Canada. It's a topographical extension of Niagara

Falls that connects the high ground above the Falls to the lower flat plain extending north to the shores of Lake Ontario.

I'd conveniently forgotten this blissful downhill stretch at the beginning of my ride four hours earlier. Halfway back up the escarpment, my legs were on fire and my heart was pounding. As my speed declined, I downshifted one, two, three times until I hit the lowest gear. The bike jerked side to side under my grinding motion. My momentum wilted and I clutched the handlebar grips, straining to stay balanced with each labored push forward. Despite the cool breeze behind me, my sweat-soaked cotton T-shirt clung to my back. With a grunt and one final push, I made it to the top. I stood straddling my bike, arms draped over the handlebars and gasping for breath. A new thought entered my mind: "I'll bet Alaska has hills, and I'll bet they're longer and steeper than this one." I hadn't thought about hills before. My fear needle took another jump.

My red Fuji bike.

A new thought entered my mind: "I'll bet Alaska has hills, and I'll bet they're longer and steeper than this one."

"Bicyclese"

As a seasoned strategist, I knew there must be a solution to the glaring skepticism and doubt that now filled my mind. Technology—that was the answer! I needed a new bike that would somehow defy gravity in its easy ascent of the steepest hills. The bike would transform me from the lumbering hulk of my test ride to a lean athlete skimming across the pavement like a pelican gliding effortlessly over the ocean surface. The search was on.

Before heading to the Yellow Pages for a list of local bike shops, I needed to bolster my below-basic knowledge of bicycles. Without better depth, I would resemble a first-time car buyer walking into a showroom and announcing, "I want to buy a car." When the inevitable response came from the badly dressed salesman inquiring as to how much horsepower, cloth or leather, standard or automatic, SUV or sedan, I would be left speechless, not knowing the meaning of any of these odd terms. Clearly, some bicycle research was an essential prerequisite to any bike shop visits.

I started with the May issue of *Bicycling* magazine, a gift from Ted. I was amazed. This was my first glimpse of a distinct substrata of our society—the "Bicycle People." We're all well aware of the larger segment of our society that shares a mania for the game of golf. These people spend endless hours reading golf magazines; telling golf stories, usually laced with slang expressions like "crushed it," drained it," or "in a groove"; and searching for the new technology that will carry a twenty-two handicapper to that promised land of single digits. They speak their own techno-language, spotted with words and phrases like "torque," "over-the-top," "square grooves," and "cavity-backed." They debate at length the benefits of titanium versus steel heads and solid core versus wound balls. Even dimple patterns can dominate a nineteenth hole (that's the bar) discussion.

While fewer in number and far less visible, the bicycling aficionados live in a world that is equally characterized by their own vocabulary and debates about new technologies. As I leafed through those pages of *Bicycling*, it dawned on me that I was on the outside looking in. And by signing up to do the ride, I was effectively committing to become a member, at least temporarily, of this newly discovered segment of our population. I also realized that I would have to start by learning to speak "Bicyclese," as most of the articles in the magazine made no more sense to me than random excerpts from the New England Journal of Medicine. Expressions like "drops," "crankset," "aero bars," "cassette," and "honking" regularly tripped my comprehension and frustrated my progress. I determined to seek a mentor to guide my passage into this strange world of bicyclers.

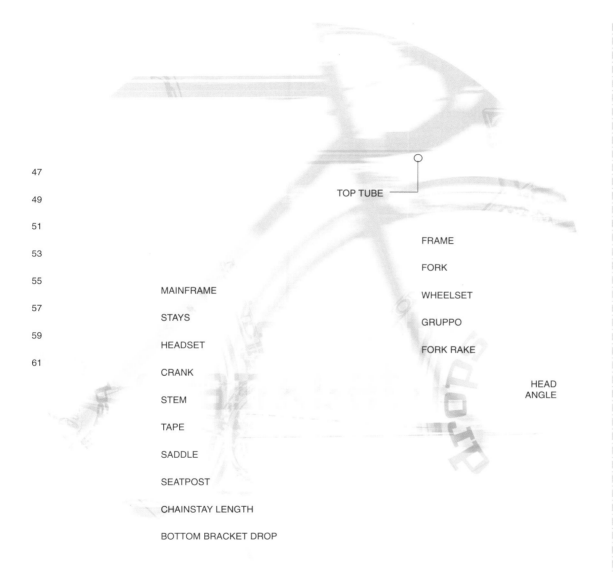

47

49

51

53

55

57

59

61

MAINFRAME

STAYS

HEADSET

CRANK

STEM

TAPE

SADDLE

SEATPOST

CHAINSTAY LENGTH

BOTTOM BRACKET DROP

TOP TUBE

FRAME

FORK

WHEELSET

GRUPPO

FORK RAKE

HEAD
ANGLE

I needed a new bike that would somehow defy gravity in its easy ascent of the steepest hills.

The King Rider

The package of information on the ride included the name, telephone number, and e-mail address of a contact representative from Pallotta Team-Works, the company that orchestrated the ride. In case I had any questions about anything related to the ride, this was the person to call. My contact's name was Nick King, also known by his e-mail address as the "King Rider." The next stop on my research circuit was a call to Nick to ask general questions about the event, but mostly to find out what I should be looking for when I ventured out shopping for my new bike.

My call went to the Pallotta switchboard and was passed immediately to Nick, who picked up on the first ring. "Hey, this is Nick," he said, launching our half-hour conversation. I've communicated more easily with Portuguese cab drivers. Here I was, a forty-eight-year-old businessman in Buffalo, chatting with a California-based bicycle zealot who was born a half decade after I passed that bar exam.

Bringing to bear my well-honed business skills in managing relationships, I quickly introduced myself and returned the subject to Nick and his background. Asking people to talk about themselves is a fail-safe method to establish a rapport. Nick was happy to oblige. Without a moment's hesitation, he declared, "I'd be happy the rest of my life with a dry place to sleep, my dog, and a good bike."

That was my first clue that Nick and I may not be occupying the same orbit. Somewhat at a loss by his straight-up response, I stammered back an awkward half question, half statement about it not sounding like he was a married man. He confirmed that was the case and offered that although he liked women, he couldn't rank them up there with his dog or bike. I decided it was time to move on to the point of my call.

With pad and pen ready, I asked Nick, "What kind of bike should I buy to make this trip as easy as possible?"

It was a carefully phrased question that I had prepared in

elektraVision/PictureQuest

advance. Nick jumped on this subject like his dog on a juicy bone. At the end of his thirty-minute monologue, my pad was still blank and my head was swimming. His discourse was littered with lengthy courses on the pros and cons of different types of forks, lengths of stems, and quality of components. I was too flustered to interrupt and advise him that to me, a fork is on a napkin or in a road, and a stem is invariably found in a garden, not on a bicycle.

Without time or humility to circle back to the start of our conversation, I thanked Nick, promised insincerely to stay in touch, and said "so long."

Nick said, "That's cool, man," and no doubt headed off in the direction of his dog, his bike, or both. I was still lost in the bicycle wilderness. My fear needle took yet another jump.

"I'd be happy the rest of my life with a dry place to sleep, a dog, and a good bike."

25

Handlebars

With my advance research going nowhere, it was time to move on. Next step, the Yellow Pages. I quickly narrowed the prospects down to six bike shops—the six who bought quarter- or half-page ads along with their listings in the Yellow Pages. I theorized that a shop that could afford an ad must be more reputable or knowledgeable than the others.

My next cull was based on how many exotic-sounding brands each shop claimed to represent. I discounted any shops with "Schwinn" in their ads because, rightly or wrongly, I equated Schwinn with the slow, bulky, fat-tired bike I had in the late '50s, about the same era my mother had a Plymouth automobile with similar features. Any ads that included Huffy bikes were similarly scratched because the name reminded me of the awful sound from my heaving lungs during my test ride. Clearly a Schwinn or a Huffy would not carry me effortlessly across Alaska. I needed something with a more exotic image—like a sleek Italian Bianchi or a brawny American Trek.

Over the next week, I managed to visit all six bike shops on my final list. Bike shops two through six each gave me strikingly different advice, supported by different theories. Each shop also tried to sell me a different type of bike, ranging from a high-end hybrid bike ("It'll be more comfortable") to an aluminum racing bike ("It will get you there faster"). While these varying opinions led me to no easy conclusions, they did serve to educate me just enough to be conversant.

I headed back to the first shop for one reason. It was the only shop where they didn't try to sell me a bike. Jim Costello, the co-owner of Handlebars (catchy name) insisted that he couldn't recommend a bike for me until he did a fitting. Again I was stumped, since my last fitting was for a custom suit that I'd purchased ten years ago when people still wore suits. Sensing my naive confusion, Jim explained it to me in the pleasant but slightly impatient tone that parents might use to dissuade their toddler from touching the stove: "It is critically important that you have a bike that fits your body dimensions, or you will suffer imponderable agony for most of your five hundred miles." As I definitely comprehended the concept of agony, I was a ready convert and made an appointment for my first-ever bike fitting.

Over the following two weeks, I made a half dozen visits to Jim's shop, including my fitting and the eventual purchase of my new bike. I confess that I was a little intimidated by Jim at the outset. Here was a man who was an established and respected resident of the bicycle world. Yet with each visit, I felt increasingly more comfortable and found myself loitering longer than necessary to transact my business, a rarity given my normally time-pressed mind-set.

Hidden in a mostly residential North Buffalo neighborhood, Handlebars occupied an unassuming three-story wood structure. It was an odd-shaped, '50s design with a heavy mansard roof that descended like an eyelid closing over the front façade. The "Handlebars" sign above the entrance was obscured by a row of young maple trees evenly spaced along the curb. If not for the small bike rack out front, you could easily pass by the shop for years without knowing it was there.

Entering the shop, you could sense an atmosphere akin to an old country store. As the wooden front door swung in, a bell (not a buzzer) rang, alerting Jim or his partner, Peter Depagter, to your arrival. With one step inside, you would be engulfed in tight rows of multicolored, glistening road bikes. A line of teal blue Bianchis occupied the

Handlebars Cycle Co.

Clearly a Schwinn or a Huffy would not carry me effortlessly across Alaska. I needed something with a more exotic image— like a sleek Italian Bianchi or a brawny American Trek.

center of the main shop floor, while double decker rows of black, yellow, red, and white Trek and LeMond bikes lined the right and rear walls. In a small nook just inside to the left was the clothes section. No more than eight by ten feet, it was jammed with racks of bike clothes and low-slung wall shelves bearing a variety of multicolored bike shoes.

Above the bikes on the rear wall was a television and VCR playing a continuous loop of bicycle road races, like the Tour de France. The low sound served only as background noise for the nonstop banter of the shop's inhabitants. The heart of the shop was in the back left quarter, where Jim, Peter, and often a part-time helper were always at work. In a Santa's workshop atmosphere, their hands and tools moved mechanically, but in an unhurried fashion, as they assembled and repaired the road bikes that flowed through their business.

Clad in his canvas apron, Jim could reach into one of its

several pockets and always find on the first try the exact tool he needed to make the next adjustment. Underneath the apron, he wore a T-shirt, loose-fitting shorts, black sneakers, and short black socks. At first impression, his most distinguishing characteristic was his clean-shaven head, which was set off by dark sideburns and pierced earrings in both ears. He was short but sturdily built. Still in his early thirties, his muscled calves and quads gave credence to his career as a professional racer.

After my first couple visits, I became accustomed to Jim's "unconventional" look, and only then did I take greater note of his other traits. Exchanging verbal barbs and stories with his coworkers and clientele, his wit and intelligence were ever present. While deferential to Peter, Jim was clearly the man in charge. His manner was nonchalant, but he was all business as he fielded phone calls, worked on bikes, and waited on customers. It was a daily clinic of multitasking, but despite the volume of activity, Jim never seemed frazzled or even hurried.

Blended with his intelligence and talent was an important streak of compassion. On one of my many visits to the shop, Jim was assembling a new bike for an eighteen-year-old boy who was trying to ride across the country. Somewhere near Buffalo, he had an accident. He escaped with minor injuries, but the bike was totaled. The boy was in the shop, looking very alone and dispirited. His savings were low, and now he needed a

Jim Costello and Peter Depagter, proprietors of Handlebars.

new bike. Not only did Jim give him a good price on a new bike, but also he stayed in the shop, assembling the bike well into the evening so the boy would be able to continue his trek in the morning.

Both Jim and I knew early in our first conversation that I was a biking neophyte, so I didn't bother with any pretenses. I needed fast help, and I put myself at his mercy. It was the best decision of my preride preparations. Over the next three months, I made numerous visits to Handlebars, many times simply seeking advice on training or riding technique.

Jim was exactly what I needed. When I returned to

Handlebars after my survey of the other local shops, Jim took great care (and over two hours) to develop the right fitting for my bike. Once that was done, the process of selecting a bike, pedals, shoes, and components took less than half an hour. My most difficult decision was the color of the handlebar tape. Overcoming my automatic leaning toward the conservative, inconspicuous black, I opted at Jim's urging for a bold gold color to match the trim on my new bike. It was perhaps my first small step across the line into the bicycle subculture.

Four days later, I returned to claim my new bike—a sleek LeMond Buenos Aires, made by Trek. My excitement level was rising and my family took notice. Here was their fairly normal, conservative, serious husband/dad getting giddy over his new bicycle. I deservedly earned the nickname "Cycle-boy" at home and was the butt of numerous jokes, but I didn't care. I was becoming a new man with a new bike.

My excitement level was rising and my family took notice. Here was their fairly normal, conservative, serious husband/dad getting giddy over his new bicycle.

I deservedly earned the nickname "Cycle-boy" at home and was the butt of numerous jokes, but I didn't care.

I was becoming a new man with a new bike.

The Bike

My new bike did make a difference. All that money, all those measurements, and all those high-tech components do make it easier to ride. Certainly the most challenging change was the switch to Speedplay pedals, which clip onto the fasteners attached to the bottom of my new bicycle shoes that cost more than my last two pairs of loafers from Allen Edmonds. Any skepticism about the need for bike shoes and clipless pedals was erased when I read in one of my bike books that they would increase the efficiency of my pedaling by about 30 percent. The same book also cautioned about the need to get used to having your feet physically locked to your pedals. If you have to stop quickly, you'd better remember to exit the clips, or you'll tilt over sideways in a slow-motion exhibition that borders on slapstick comedy. The key to a safe stop is to click your heels out sideways then lift up to exit. Every time I did it, I felt like Dorothy trying to get home from Oz.

My first few stops were cleanly executed, but some-

how I knew my time would come. Based on the lore provided by the regulars at Handlebars, everybody forgets to click out at least once. I didn't doubt this truth, but I hoped my time would not occur between two trucks stopped at a railroad crossing. (Note to self: Stay away from trucks.)

With all the great features and benefits of my new ride, there had to be at least one downside. It didn't take me long to find it—my seat, or as they say in Bicyclese, my "saddle." Everything about my new bike made sense except the saddle. You want a bike to be light, so you can go faster. You want the gears to be smooth, so you can adjust speeds without losing momentum. However, for some reason, I was supposed to want my saddle to be narrow, small, and hard.

Jim and others told me early on that I would eventually get used to my saddle. After suffering through my first two hundred miles, I still felt like I was sitting on top of a flag pole—sometimes one of those flag poles with the decorative eagle on top. Being a rookie in the bicycle world, I was not about to challenge the wisdom of the saddle design. Contributing to my willingness to have faith was the fact that Mary and I didn't intend to have any more children. I'm not sure whether the saddle gradually formed to my anatomy or vice versa, but by mid-June I was able to ride for six hours a day with little discomfort.

After suffering through my first two hundred miles, I still felt like I was sitting on top of a flag pole. . . .

31

Training

Time in the Saddle

Grand Island, New York

Even before the purchase of my bike, I had bought two books and four magazines that included training routines for long-distance biking. I was seeking that fail-safe routine that would quickly and easily put me in shape to ride ninety to one hundred miles a day for six days in a row. I stopped looking because all the training programs were basically the same: you have to ride a lot of miles to get ready to ride a lot of miles. I could have saved myself the cost of those books by listening to Jim. When asked about a good training regimen for the ride, his four-word response was "Time in the saddle."

Since most long-distance training programs are built around a six-month time frame, I at least knew I was starting late. I would have to compress a six-month program into three. I figured if I spent 80 percent of my waking hours on the bike, I could get it all in. And by the way, stationary bikes don't really count. You have to feel the wind and the potholes to prepare for the real thing.

My goal for June was to average one hundred miles per week. All of my training rides were around western New York where I live and work. I quickly learned that route research is a must. Some roads present far more dangers than others, and I gained new appreciation for those municipalities that provide wide shoulders on their roadways. Without them, biking transforms from invigorating exercise to panicky survival. Every bicyclist has experienced that inevitable moment when you feel an angry pickup truck bearing down over your left shoulder just as you are fast approaching that sewer grate twenty feet dead ahead.

After careful consideration, I selected Grand Island for my first major outing. It sits in the middle of the Niagara River and is sparsely populated, very flat, and ringed by a well-paved twenty-mile roadway. I attached my bike rack to the back of my car, carefully positioned my new lightweight LeMond, and backed out of my driveway for the fifteen-minute drive to Grand Island.

One of the most important virtues of this new bike is its weight—just about twenty pounds. Merging onto the expressway and accelerating to fifty miles per hour, I glanced into the rearview mirror and was horrified to see my pristine new treasure floating up on the edge of the rack rails, ready to take flight. Only a screeching halt on the shoulder of I-190 aborted this disastrous takeoff. As I secured the bike firmly to the rack with elastic cords, I pondered how close I had come to demolishing my new bike before my first ride. None of the bike books warned against the perils of failing to tie down the lightweight road bikes to your car rack. I presumed this insight was too obvious even for the novice. Where did that place me?

There were more learnings to come. My second run-in with the "too-obvious" lessons came on my very next outing. After driving east to the city outskirts, I parked on Main Street in Clarence and headed farther east on my bike. After twenty-five miles of dodging traffic and seeking alternative side routes, I returned to where I thought I had started. In my enthusiasm to start my ride, I had forgotten where I parked my car. As I rode up and down Main Street, everything looked familiar, but I couldn't recall whether I was in my car or on my bike when I saw the various landmarks. An hour later, after ten more miles of backtracking and back-backtracking, I found it. I doubt whether Noah felt more relieved when he first spotted land after the great flood.

Over the next few weeks, my rides took me more into the rural areas, especially south of the city. While there is thankfully less traffic in this region, the ghastly sight of mangled animal life along the roadside prevented me from becoming careless. At first, I thought the carnage on the pavement must be an aberration, just a bad luck stretch of road for the animal kingdom. Not so. The bodies were unending throughout the rural regions. The heavy toll of flattened and disfigured wildlife ranged from tiny field mice to toads to fully grown deer. Even a number of slow-winged birds fell victim to the relentless barrage of traffic.

As a motorist I had been oblivious to these fatalities. Like most drivers, I was too busy changing the radio station, yelling at my son in the backseat, or talking on the phone. Now as a bicyclist, I became fixated on the road, and each individual carcass became a clarion of warning. As a nonmotorized traveler on these roads, I found myself identifying more with the animals than the motorists. It's a war out there, and the enemy is bigger, more powerful, and unconcerned about my welfare.

Every bicyclist has experienced that inevitable moment when you feel an angry pickup truck bearing down over your left shoulder just as you are fast approaching that sewer grate twenty feet dead ahead.

And Even a Few Bears

Pallotta TeamWorks, which organized the Alaska ride, generated a continuous stream of e-mails and mailings to all the registered riders, including a newsletter called the *VacScene*. While most of these mass communications were designed to support and encourage the fund-raising efforts, occasionally they would sprinkle in one or two insights into the ride itself. One of the *VacScene*s arrived the second week of June. Just as my confidence was starting to take shape, it all came apart on the third page of the newsletter. A short article describing the ride was laced with phrases like, "extremely challenging terrain," "very inconsistent road conditions," "long stretches of uphill climbs," and "bears." The bears were the least of my concerns. I'd take the bears and add lions, tigers, and even a rattlesnake in return for a flat, well-paved road. But lacking the ability to reverse the impact of continental drift on the Alaska terrain, I would have to face a new reality. The long distances were no longer the primary foe. Now I had to add the challenging terrain and the bad road conditions to my list of worries.

Ted called me at work the next day. "Did you read the newsletter?" he asked. Ted had zeroed in on exactly the same phrases. There was consolation in having a friend to share my fears.

As we talked on, our exchanges of mutual concern turned to paranoia. "It feels like they're luring us in," I said to Ted.

"Yeah," he replied, "they wait 'til we buy these expensive new bikes, then they give us the gory details." Ted decided it was time to call Nick King (the King Rider) to squeeze the truth out of him.

At seven the next morning, Ted pulled his dark green Jeep Cherokee into my driveway. It was a clear, sun-drenched early summer day, perfect for a long training ride. With no traffic on the roads, Ted quickly navigated the city streets, and we were on the thruway heading south when we picked up on our previous day's conversation and Ted's follow-up call to Nick.

"Nick said he thinks we're both whining too much," Ted reported. "He said those newsletters are just meant to keep all the riders motivated to train."

"Well, they've certainly got my attention," I shot back.

"What worries me is that Nick's comments don't seem consistent with what I heard from the guy who did the ride last year." Ted had managed to track down a participant in the 2000 Alaska ride who was from Buffalo. He had confessed to Ted that it was "very tough," and he was among a small percentage of people who managed to complete the entire ride. The conditions were so severe that he resorted to wrapping his shoes and helmet with duct tape in a desperate attempt to keep warm and dry.

Having shared this conversation over the dinner table at home, Ted said that his wife, Ginna, was questioning our sanity. "She thinks we're in over our heads," he admitted.

"She might be right," I conceded. "How can we believe Nick when he didn't even go on the Alaska ride last year?"

Twenty minutes later, we were parking on Main Street in the village of East Aurora. This quaint community became the launch point for my favorite rides over the course of the summer. East Aurora lies southeast of Buffalo at the edge of Erie County. The highway leading in is straight and flat, but beyond the town the landscape transforms into a series of ridges and valleys stretching east to the Finger Lakes.

VacScene

THE OFFICIAL NEWSLETTER OF THE PALLOTTA TEAMWORKS AIDS VACCINE RIDES / APRIL 2001

Montana
July 30 – August 5, 2001
Missoula to Billings
7 days
575 miles

Alaska
August 20-25, 2001
Fairbanks to Anchorage
6 days
500 miles

Canada⊃U.S.
September 5-9, 2001
Montreal to Portland, Maine
5 days
400 miles

Invite your friends to ride!

The essence of the Pallotta TeamWorks AIDS Vaccine Rides is the enthusiasm and awe-inspiring willingness of the riders and crew. Deep within each rider or crew member is an innate resolve and determination that rises up and takes hold. It is a determination to work and ride in the face of exhaustion, irritation, and seemingly impossible odds. Those impossible odds suddenly become less daunting when we stand and work together. Through this spirit of unity, the battle against AIDS will be won.

We invite you to share the indomitable spirit of the AIDS Vaccine Rides with your friends and loved ones. Imagine what could be if everyone who is already registered for the Ride brought along one friend. Imagine if everyone brought two friends . . . three friends, four friends. Or, imagine if your friend brought along a friend and your friend's friend brought along a friend and so on and so on and so on. Imagine the power and awareness that would be generated by the sheer number of people uniting together to find a cure for AIDS.

Those who can't imagine might think, "I'm already doing enough." Well, we haven't done enough until the 13.2 million children in Africa who have lost their parents to AIDS are placed in new homes with loving families. In the time it takes you to even read this article, 11 more people will have been infected with HIV. We haven't done enough until you can read that and know that not one more person has been infected with HIV. We haven't done enough until not one more person dies from AIDS. We haven't done enough until we have a vaccine, a cure for AIDS.

Riders and crew, you have an opportunity to truly "Make AIDS History" not just in your personal training and fundraising, but to significantly increase the odds for success by bringing others along with you. Register them now— don't wait another minute. Your impact can start immediately. Share the Ride today! Share the spirit today! Just imagine what could happen if you did.

John Lennon's celebrated lyrics say it best, "Imagine all the people sharing all the world." Well, imagine all the people sharing the Pallotta TeamWorks AIDS Vaccine Rides. Tell your friends to register on the website at www.vaccineride.org or call (888) 553-4567 today!

Pallotta TeamWorks. | **Impossible.dreams.**
Creators and Producers of the AIDS Vaccine Rides

Contact:

AIDS Vaccine Ride Office
P.O. Box 480128
Los Angeles, CA 90048

(323) 857-7222 local
(888) 553-4567 toll-free
(323) 857-0902 facsimile
www.vaccineride.org

A short article describing the ride was laced with phrases like, "extremely challenging terrain," "very inconsistent road conditions," "long stretches of uphill climbs," and "bears."

Aptly named, the Finger Lakes are a series of long, narrow, fingerlike freshwater lakes lined up across the central part of New York State. Seneca and Cayuga are the largest of these lakes, which all bear the names of the Native Americans who lived in this bountiful region long before the arrival of settlers from Europe. The Finger Lakes were formed over 500 million years ago during the Pleistocene Ice Age. Enormous glaciers gouged deep furrows in the terrain as they pushed south over the landscape. When they later receded north, the ice melted, leaving these extraordinary deep, narrow lakes. This same geological phenomenon also sculpted the rows of narrow north-south valleys across which I conducted much of my preride training.

After a few minutes of token stretching, Ted and I rode out of East Aurora on Route 20A. With the rising sun in our faces, we tackled the first of the series of climbs on our way to Warsaw, about twenty-five miles due east. We soon crossed from Erie into Wyoming County, where most of our ride would take place. The well-maintained country roads of Wyoming County roll through rural scenes of dairy farms and knee-high fields of corn, interrupted every eight or ten miles by another small town, usually no more than a few faded homes clustered around a crossroads. Only the town of Attica on the northern edge of the county retains some broad notoriety. The harsh violent images brought to mind by the uprising in the Attica Correctional Facility are a disturbing contrast to the pastoral sameness and quietude of the rest of Wyoming County.

Our route on this day did not go near Attica but instead looped south and back west through Wethersfield Springs, North Java, and Strykersville. Arriving back in Erie County in the town of Holland, we saw a sign for Vermont Hill Road and decided to take it. After starting off as a gentle incline, it morphed into a series of steep switchbacks climbing out of the valley. Long before the top, we had both shifted to the lowest of our twenty-one gears.

Hill climbing on a bicycle has one special distinction. Unlike hikers or runners, who can stop and rest part way up a steep hill, bikers have to make it up nonstop. Once you stop, you cannot restart going up an incline, and you face the unpleasant choice of riding down to the bottom for another try or disembarking and walking your bike the rest of the way up the hill.

Not liking either of these alternatives, Ted and I kept grinding the pedals forward in our jerky, desperate motion. Turning the corner on the final switchback, we arrived at the top, hyperventilating and wincing from the fiery pain in our thigh muscles. Draped over the front of my bike, trying to catch my breath, I exchanged a look with Ted. We couldn't speak, but we didn't need to. We were both thinking the same thing. We were not ready for Alaska.

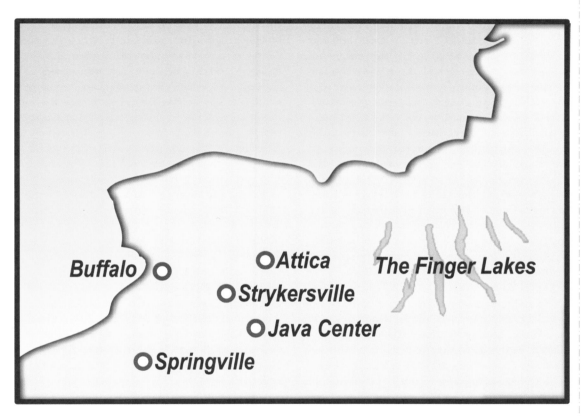

Some towns on my training routes.

Draped over the front of my bike, trying to catch my breath, I exchanged a look with Ted. We couldn't speak, but we didn't need to. We were both thinking the same thing. We were not ready for Alaska.

Earthquake

The following week, I received a call from George Kreiner inviting Ted and me to join him for a ride on Sunday in Canada just across the border from Buffalo. Ted and I met up with George and his son Will on the outskirts of Port Colborne, and the four of us headed west into a cool, gray day along the northern shores of Lake Erie. Will jumped out in front and set a pace with his twenty-five-year-old legs that was unfamiliar to Ted and me. After less than a mile, I was ready to admit my inability to sustain this pace when George came to our aid. He explained how we could draft to stay up with Will. Drafting, a technique used in biking, running, and motor racing, is accomplished by positioning oneself close behind another participant, which reduces wind resistance and enables greater speed with less effort. George demonstrated the technique by pulling up to within a few inches of Will's rear wheel.

George Kreiner at age fifty-two is still a fine athlete. After excelling in hockey and football at Nichols School, he went on to captain the University of Vermont hockey team. As a hard-hitting defenseman, George was dubbed "Earthquake" by the Vermont press. Although known for his toughness and affable nature, he also became infamous in the years to come for his mishaps. In a variety of sports, as well as nonathletic activities, George has suffered breaks, tears, strains, and contusions across the whole of his anatomy. He once commented to me that getting divorced was "like having your arms pulled off without any anesthetic." Coming from George, I thought at the time, the analogy was not entirely figurative. Somewhere along the way, his Earthquake moniker gave way to a less subtle but more updated nickname—"Crash Kreiner."

Although still an avid squash player, golfer, and fisherman, road bicycling had become a primary passion for George in recent years. As in all his endeavors, he brought a competitive spirit to his bicycling. For George, it was more a vocation than a weekend hobby. He has studied the sport assiduously and become a knowledgeable resource on everything from equipment to riding technique. Like Ted and me, George was training for a five-hundred-mile ride, but his jaunt was to take place across the Continental Divide in late July. Knowing that Ted and I were two newcomers to the sport, George was eager to share his bicycling knowledge with us during this Sunday morning ride.

Having eased in just a breath behind Will, George motioned for me to follow in place behind him and then Ted similarly behind me in the fourth position. I was thrilled to be part of my first peloton—that's Bicyclese for a line of bicyclers riding so closely together they appear to be linked components of a long multiwheeled vehicle. I thought about the liquid flowing images of the pelotons I had watched on the video at Handlebars, and I smiled smugly that I was now helping to create a similar image along this lakeshore route. I wanted to look up to see the local residents admiring our collective form, but I stayed nervously focused on George's rear wheel just inches ahead.

Although Will picked up the pace to twenty-four miles per hour, the drafting phenomenon made it easy for us to stay with him. As we sailed along mile after mile, I became increasingly comfortable with the inherent risk of being so close together.

I was concluding that drafting would be the secret weapon to get across Alaska when George moved up a hair too much and his front wheel clipped Will's rear tire. The next few seconds were akin to those oft-

George on a bike trip in Montana.

repeated reruns of NASCAR crashes when one car innocently nips the rear of another and is somehow catapulted, twisting out of control. George and his bike went airborne, rotated sideways, and crashed to the pavement with a screeching of steel on concrete. As George's tragic flight unfolded in the airspace just before me, I was sure to be next, and I waited in slow motion for my own upending. I was saved only by the rotation that carried George's bike just a few inches to my left. As the friction of steel on concrete slowed his forward slide, my front wheel brushed the edge of his flattened rear tire. Fiercely gripping the handlebars, I stayed upright and guided myself quivering into the shallow ravine by the roadside.

Ted was saved by an amazing coincidence—just seconds before the accident, he had blown out a tire and was already slowing down. It was not our time.

George lay across the center line of the two-lane road, his feet still attached to his pedals. His helmet was shattered, and there was a twenty-foot-long red streak on the pavement leading up to where he lay. Our immediate fears of a bloody head injury were unfounded. The red streak was the remnants of nylon material from his left riding glove, which had scraped along the concrete. Except for some road rash and the early signs of severe soreness, George was unharmed.

The hair-raising sound of the accident brought out the local residents, who, instead of admiring our peloton, offered ice and other forms of assistance. After a remarkably brief recovery, George was back on his bike, already reminiscing about this latest chapter in his anthology of accidents. No broken bones, but Crash Kreiner had revalidated his nickname one more time.

As we reviewed our weekend of new bicycling experience, Ted and I deposited one more learning to our knowledge bank: high-speed drafting was not for amateurs.

George and his bike went airborne, rotated sideways, and crashed to the pavement with a screeching of steel on concrete.

12

Tour de Cure

The Buffalo-area Tour de Cure fund-raiser annually attracts over 1,000 bicyclists.

My Canada excursion with George and Will Kreiner and Ted was the largest group ride I'd experienced to date. Given the near disaster of that ride and the fact that the Alaska trip would include over a thousand riders, I decided I'd better learn to ride in a crowd.

My first outing in an organized bicycle event was the Tour de Cure, a nationwide fund-raiser for diabetes research. The Buffalo-area event is always the largest in the country, and this year was no exception, with more than two thousand riders.

Since Ted was away at Williams College watching his daughter Liza graduate, I had arranged to meet up with the Kreiners and a few others to tackle the sixty-two-mile section of the Tour de Cure.

Arriving at the Ellicott Creek Park starting area among the throngs of participants, I was interested to discover more nuances of the bicycle culture. As a sporting event, an organized bike race has much in common with an Elizabethan-era foxhunt with its parade of red-coated huntsmen sitting erect in their saddles. The prerace crowd of Tour de Cure riders was decked out in their finery of bicycle wear. The common fashion thrust was bright colors and wild designs. Bicyclists must be a patriotic lot, as the favorite design theme was certainly red, white, and blue variations of the American flag.

As I stood there surveying this colorful crowd, I was surprised by this large number of serious bicyclers in the western New York area. But there they were, in all their bright plumage. And there I was, in black—shirt, pants, shoes—all black. I was thankful that my helmet was a pleasing royal blue, but even that was an accident. I had pilfered the helmet from my daughter, Hanna, because mine was lost in the garage. Yes, my own helmet was black. I admitted I had always been a fairly conservative dresser, but now I was a bicycler. I made a mental note, "Buy a wild-looking jersey," even though I'd be subjected to painful teasing from Mary and the kids.

Shortly before 8 a.m., the fifty-plus participants in the sixty-two mile segment collected at the starting line. While it was not officially a race, everyone was still jockeying for position near the front of the pack. I was engaged in some nervous chatter with those around me when the clock struck eight and I received yet another lesson—sometimes a cannon is used to start these races. Unprepared as I was, the concussion of the blast almost blew me over, and I was momentarily paralyzed as the pack surged forward around me. So much for a good start.

Beyond that dubious beginning, it was a rewarding introduction to a large group event. During the course of the ride and the periodic rest stops, I found myself included in four or more different groupings. At the end I was somehow back with the Kreiners, whom I had lost from sight in the confusion of the start. We finished in just over three hours, averaging about nineteen miles per hour.

The opportunity to draft behind a line of faster riders was the major contributor to my own speed. Yet this technique was also stressful, as I had to concentrate continuously on the rear wheel of the rider just inches ahead of me. This singular focus rendered me oblivious to the surroundings. I could have ridden down the Las Vegas strip and have never seen a neon sign. I was doubting that the benefits of peloton riding were worth the toll on the overall experience.

Learning the technical nuances of riding with a large group was my expected takeaway from the Tour de Cure, but there was more. The subtle competitiveness that urged everyone on was oddly blended with an even more palpable sense of camaraderie. It was a modern-day Hans Christian Andersen story, where the young boy leading the big ice skating race across the frozen lake turns back to aid a rival who has fallen through the ice. I came to learn that bicyclists have the same compassion and concern for fellow riders, albeit complete strangers. This trait further warmed me to the sport.

An organized bike race has much in common with an Elizabethan-era foxhunt with its parade of red-coated huntsmen sitting erect in their saddles.

43

13

Oh, Deer

As early summer passed, I was reserving every Saturday and Sunday for training rides. On one gray and threatening Saturday morning, I traveled again to East Aurora to train in the hilly terrain of the southern tier. Heading east on Route 20A, I struggled up and over the now-familiar inclines on my way to Warsaw. On each hill, my thoughts projected to the day in Alaska when we would face a single hill that measured more than five miles in length. None of the pitches on Route 20A were even one mile long, and I was still hyperventilating as I reached the summit of each one. I wondered how much better my conditioning could get with only two months to go. I was doubtful.

My return trip was the more southern route on deserted country roads that link the tiny towns in each valley bottom. Between the towns were acres of crops and periodic dairy farms with the ever-present "Got Milk?" logo painted on a barn or shed. The easier hills allowed me to better contemplate the pleasant surroundings and enjoy the rural solitude.

Heading back north for my final ten miles, the sky darkened with heavy black clouds. Moments later, the heavens opened up, the road became a riverbed, and my visibility was nil. Consider the feeling of driving your car down a road at twenty miles per hour in a torrential downpour with your head out the window. The drops were heavy and seemed to explode as they hit my cheeks and glasses.

As I was accepting the hopelessness of continuing on, I spotted a farmer's school bus shelter just ahead. These tiny sheds protect the children from cold winter winds as they wait near the road for the school bus to arrive. I used this one to escape the driving rain. I was doubly lucky with my cell phone call to good friend John Mineo. John, who lives in East Aurora, picked up on the first ring. Fifteen minutes later, he and his SUV were there to rescue me.

Sunday, in contrast, was a clear, sunny morning. I headed north from my home, riding along the Niagara River up into flatlands of Niagara County. After two hours, I turned back south on a sparsely traveled two-lane, wide-shouldered road carving through vineyards and open fields.

I felt strong. Lost in thought, I was at my peak cruising speed of about twenty-two miles per hour when I was startled by a sudden motion in front to my left. A deer had shot out of the vineyard on the other side of the road and was coming straight across on a sure collision course with me and my bike. Within the same second, I was passed by a car cruising over fifty miles an hour.

The car, the deer, and I were the only moving objects within a square mile, yet here we all were improbably converging on the same point. The deer was bounding but failed to get across before the onrushing car bumper struck the deer's right hindquarter with a sickening thud.

The low force of the car lifted the stricken animal into the air and propelled it in a wild cartwheeling arc directly over my head. It passed so close I could feel the rush of air on the back of my neck as the deer's body sailed up and over. The deer landed with a second thud on its side in an open field more than thirty feet to my right.

I finally stopped just in time to see the animal thrash

In the final stages of training, I was spending up to eighteen hours a week in the saddle.

The low force of the car lifted the stricken animal into the air and propelled it in a wild cartwheeling arc directly over my head. It passed so close I could feel the rush of air on the back of my neck as the deer's body sailed up and over. . . . I was left alone by the side of the road, trying to grasp this surreal sequence of events.

about on its back, then amazingly the deer was on its feet and disappeared into the brush beyond. The car never stopped to check on either of the other two actors in this bizarre rural road drama. A moment later, both the deer and the car were out of sight, and the quiet solitude was restored.

I was left alone by the side of the road, trying to grasp this surreal sequence of events. I wanted to turn to someone and say, "Did you see what just happened?!" No one was there, so I shook my head in silent disbelief and continued on my way.

14

Not to Worry . . .
There's Always the Force

At least once a week after I registered for the Alaska ride, I would receive an e-mail from my ride guide, the King Rider. His communication objectives were basically threefold: first, to encourage our fund-raising; second, to encourage our training (he didn't want to have to push us all up that five-mile hill); and third, to lace his messages with just enough optimism that we didn't all change our minds and go sit on a beach instead of joining him in Alaska. As the reality of five hundred miles sunk in, our initial enthusiasm was, in fact, wilting under the heat of the relentless training routine. Nick King's repeated efforts to kindle our spirits reached new heights of creativity and desperation in one late June e-mail. He finished his message with:

"Size matters not. Believe what you see, you must not. Believe what you cannot see, you must. Hard to do this at first. But learn to do it you must. Powerful, the Force is. Power in everything lies."

—Yoda

You may recall Yoda as the diminutive, bug-eyed, pointy-eared green fellow who mentored Luke Skywalker in one of the *Star Wars* movies. Yoda had this talent for rearranging the syntax of simple sentences to make them sound more profound. The effect was further enhanced by the mechanical crinkling of his nose and ears, as he physically emphasized his most important declarations.

I immediately called Ted and told him not to worry about training so hard because I had assurances from the King Rider that the Force would be with us. Ted said we'd better keep training just in case Darth Vader showed up on one of those hills.

I formed a mental image of the King Rider in his apartment, his dog, and his bike beside him, rewinding Yoda's soliloquy repeatedly to get this quote completely accurate. I also had no doubt I would be humming the *Star Wars* theme music on every Alaska incline on the rare chance it might attract even a wisp of the Force in my direction.

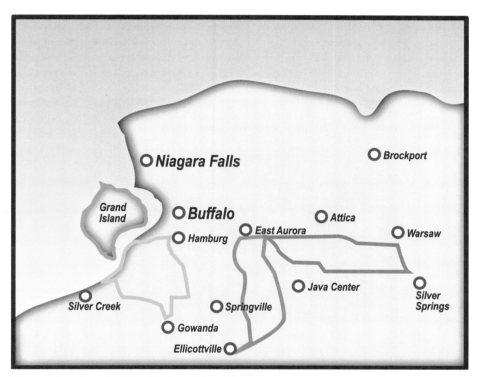

Three of our favorite New York training rides.

15

The Roswell Ride

By the end of June, Ted and I had been training for six weeks. We deemed ourselves ready for our first one-hundred-mile ride, known in Bicyclese as a "century." Several weeks earlier, we had registered to ride the 102-mile course in the Ride for Roswell, another charity fund-raising event.

Roswell Park Cancer Institute is one of the preeminent cancer research and treatment hospitals in the country, and it is thankfully located here in Buffalo. Although state-supported, the institute is constantly struggling with finances to fund the research and to advance the care of cancer patients who come here from the United States, Canada, and beyond.

The Ride for Roswell has raised over $813,000 this year for cancer research and care at Buffalo's Roswell Park Cancer Institute

The Ride for Roswell is one of a number of fund-raising events that benefit the institute. It attracts up to two thousand participants annually and generates hundreds of thousands of dollars for Roswell. Like most of the hospital's fund-raising events, the Ride for Roswell is promoted and organized by a special group of volunteers who came together in the wake of a terrible tragedy.

In 1990, a beautiful five-year-old girl named Katherine Anne Gioia succumbed to cancer. It was a tragedy that belies any sense of logic or equity. Why would God choose to take such a spirited, vivacious child so early in her life's journey? Katherine left behind a large and close-knit family.

The Gioia family has become an institution in Buffalo over the past two decades. The community has benefited from the family's leadership and support of numerous civic and charitable endeavors. Among all of the Gioias' contributions, none stands out more than their impact on Roswell Park Cancer Institute, where Katherine was treated.

Following Katherine's death, her mother, Anne Gioia, and her aunt Donna Gioia channeled their grief by founding the Roswell Park Alliance, a volunteer-run organization that financially, politically, and operationally supports the advancement of the institute. In the ensuing years, the influence and impact of the alliance have become vital elements of Roswell Park's ongoing fight against cancer.

Thousands of lives have been extended and saved due in large part to the efforts begun over ten years ago by Anne; her husband, Richard; and their family and friends. In her own way, Katherine Gioia contributed more to humanity in her short five years than most of the rest of us will accomplish over lifetimes spanning many decades.

Early on the morning of the ride, Ted and I arrived at the University of Buffalo location where the 102-mile ride was scheduled to start at 7 a.m. The temperature hovered near fifty degrees, and a frigid rain steadily fell. Without a word, we looked at each other to see if one of us was going to point out the foolishness of this endeavor. No one balked, probably because we knew we were likely to encounter similar or worse conditions in Alaska.

With little fanfare, the ride started while we were still under a tent strategizing on what to wear to stay dry. We shouldn't have bothered. Within the first mile, we were drenched, not just from the falling rain but more from the spray spitting up-ward from the fenderless wheels on our road bikes. Undaunted, we forged ahead, fol-lowing the route as it headed east along the Erie Canal, then north to the shores of Lake Ontario.

The wet conditions posed new hazards. We arrived at a bridge less than a minute after a serious accident. Spanning a small creek, the bridge consisted of a heavy metal grating with jagged edges. The surface was impossibly slippery when wet, and two riders ahead of us had lost control midway across. They both suffered deep gouges as their exposed knees and hips ground across the rough metal deck. True to form, the other riders rallied to their rescue until the medical staff arrived.

Ted and I proceeded with renewed caution. The going was slow, and the rooster-tail sprays from the rear wheels precluded any thought of drafting.

After four hours and about sixty miles, Ted's back began to ache. As the pain increased, he was forced to stop every few miles to lie down and stretch. The fourth stretch break took place on the front lawn of a pleasant rural home. The mother of the house was comfortably settled on a front porch rocking chair intermittently watching us and reading a book. All the while, the rains persisted.

From his prone position, Ted glanced at her, then turned to me and muttered, "This sucks. I want to go home."

For that brief moment, I had my only serious doubts as to whether we would actually go to Alaska. Those uncertainties were quickly erased as Ted climbed back on his bike and gutted it out for the last thirty miles.

Finally crossing the finish line some eight hours after the start, we were ecstatic to have conquered our first "century" ride. Our enthusiasm was only slightly muted by the realization that the postride celebration had long since ended. We were greeted by the few remaining volunteers, who were stacking chairs and cleaning up the parking lot. It rained all the way home.

In her own way, Katherine Gioia contributed more to humanity in her short five years than most of the rest of us will accomplish over lifetimes spanning many decades.

49

16

And the Training Goes On

A s I headed into my final month of training, I had logged over twelve hundred miles. I was amazed that I had been able to carve out the necessary time to train, mostly using early morning hours on weekdays and longer half-day rides on the weekends.

The hours were punctuated by all the experiences familiar to most road bicyclists—getting sore, getting lost, getting sworn at by angry motorists, getting chased by angrier dogs, getting hit on the nose by a large bug at twenty miles per hour, and, of course, getting flat tires, which, by necessity, I had learned how to change.

Beyond all of these somewhat distracting occurrences, I was starting to discover the subtle appeal of bicycling. I relished the sense of accomplishment after climbing a steep incline and the Disney-esque rush of fear while hurtling downhill.

But the attraction for me went beyond. A long ride developed a rhythm and a solitude that was soothing in spite of the physical exertion. It was like those early handheld movie machines where you'd turn the crank on the box to make the picture move. In cycling, you pedal perfect circles to make the scenery pass by in a smooth, continuous flow of pictures. In modern life, it is exceptionally rare to be alone, quiet, and yet focused for several hours in a row.

A long ride developed a rhythm and a solitude that was soothing in spite of the physical exertion.

17

The Ring Road

Bicycle training imposes two constant needs: time and space. As your training advances, you must seek longer, time-consuming rides to push your endurance and conditioning to the next level. But time in the saddle and distance are not enough. Training rides must also include open, less-trafficked routes where you can sustain higher cruising speeds and also practice intervals.

Intervals are a series of shorter bursts where you ride hard for a few minutes to bring your heart rate up, recover for a few minutes, and then repeat the cycle eight or ten times. Recent studies have suggested that interval training is the most effective approach to getting tuned for long-distance rides, as well as for racing.

Finding the needed time and space was a challenge for me. Living in the city, any routes outbound from my home involved at least three miles of city traffic, stop lights, potholes, and bus exhaust that contributed little benefit to my training efforts.

Frustrated by the repugnance of city street riding, I often opted to strap the bike on the back of my car and drive to the rural open spaces of Wyoming or Niagara Counties. When time was short, usually on weekdays, such trips were not an option. That's when I would head to my fall-back option, the ring road.

The City of Buffalo is blessed with one of the country's most impressive park systems. Designed by famed architect Frederick Law Olmsted in 1868, the system boasts a number of glorious circles linking spokes of wide parkways throughout the city. While insensitive city planning and the Dutch elm disease have robbed Olmsted's work of some of its original splendor, there has been a recent resurgence in the community efforts to protect and restore this distinctive reminder of Buffalo's historic prominence.

At the heart of the city and the heart of Olmsted's design is Delaware Park, originally known simply as "The Park." This 350-acre green space in the northern part of Buffalo has a rich history, from its prepark days as a camp site for War of 1812 soldiers to its prominent positioning at the southern edge of the 1901 Pan-American exposition. Olmsted's design included a man-made lake extending east to west through the middle of the green space.

The subsequent invasion in 1960 of an expressway along the north side of the lake has regrettably cut the park in half. The expressway is ironically named Scajaquada, honoring a Native American who would have certainly disapproved of the concrete disruption of this green space.

Most current-day citizens are oblivious to the intrusion of the expressway. They have never known it any other way, and they flock to both the north and south sections of the park. They come to visit the zoo, fish in the lake, or just sit and enjoy the environment. But the vast majority come to play and to exercise, especially on the northern space.

This section is ringed by a paved road, a little less than two miles in circumference. The 120 acres inside the ring teem with sports activities, ranging from rugby, baseball, soccer, and tennis to an eighteen-hole golf course, which is wedged awkwardly among the various playing fields. It's not uncommon to see an errant golfer lining up a wedge shot that must carry a youth soccer field but stop short of the ice cream stand. Tiger Woods has faced few of the unique hazards posed by the Delaware Park golf course.

In Buffalo's golden era, the ring road was an ideal

Mary captured this Delaware Park scene on a crisp fall afternoon.

The City of Buffalo is blessed with one of the country's most impressive park systems. . . . It's not uncommon to see an errant golfer lining up a wedge shot that must carry a youth soccer field but stop short of the ice cream stand.

destination for a Sunday afternoon carriage ride. Today, it attracts the increasing numbers of city dwellers in search of physical fitness or a convenient venue to shed the stress of modern life. They come in all shapes, sizes, and ages. Their modes of transportation range from walking shoes, to baby carriages, to roller blades, to scooters, and, of course, to bicycles.

Given a choice, I avoided the Ring Road as a train-ing site despite its proximity—only a half mile from my home. While car traffic has been restricted to only a quarter of the circle, the crowds of walkers, joggers, and bladers traveling in different directions at different speeds are spatially incompatible with a bicycle going twenty miles per hour. As the summer wore on and my weekly training goals increased, I was on my bike every available hour six days each week. Even after working

53

late, I could still fit in a quick trip to the ring road and add another fifteen or twenty miles to my weekly mileage log.

Such was the case one wet Wednesday evening in late July. As I drove past the park on my way home from work, I calculated that misty rain in the air would not hinder my bicycling but would persuade many of the after-work exercisers to postpone their walks or jogs to a better day. Twenty minutes later, I was entering the park on my bike and was pleased to find that my logic was accurate. Only a scattering of stern-faced joggers were spaced generously around the road.

Settling into a steady rhythm, I half-circled the park and headed toward the gradual hill on the south end of the ring. With everything in order, I reached down to adjust my new side mirror, recently acquired to replace the one I'd somehow lost in the Roswell ride. As I fidgeted with the mirror, I caught a glimpse of another rider behind me. His brightly colored, boldly lettered jersey and shorts announced his status as a serious road racer. His hands were low in the drops of his handlebars, and his torso was pitched forward to achieve maximum aerodynamics. His head was up, eyes fixed on my back. I had no doubt of his intent to use me as today's contribution to his bicycling ego.

Since my first ride in May, I had been reminding myself that I was training to ride a long and arduous route, not to win a race. Yet, as family and friends will attest, my competitive spirit, while not always visible, lies very close to the surface. I thoroughly enjoy activities in a noncompetitive atmosphere, but once challenged, I hate to lose.

Without conscious thought, that competitive instinct kicked in as this garish challenger pulled within a few feet of my rear wheel. Looking ahead to the incline of the small hill, I picked up my pace and pushed steadily toward the top. About thirty yards from the hill crest, I rose out of my saddle and used my weight to accelerate my speed up and over the hilltop.

Settling back in my saddle, I peeked back and noted my foe fifty yards behind, laboring to keep his pace. Having beaten him, I was now intent on punishment and sped off downhill to put even more distance between us. Hugging the inside curb at the north end, I started to take another look back, when just in front of me the blue plastic door of the roadside Porta-Potty swung open. Carrying too much speed to brake, I swerved enough to avoid a catastrophic direct hit, but my new side mirror was neatly cleaved off at the neck.

As I collected the broken pieces and apologized with abundance to the shaken Porta-Potty occupant, my would-be challenger passed by. My side view of his physique suggested that he had been spending significantly more time at the dessert bar than on his bike seat. Evidently, clothes don't make the man, even in the bicycle world.

Unlike skiers, it is a rare biker who dares to wear the fancy garb unless he or she has the skill to match. My brief period of triumph was effectively muted two days later, when on a return trip to the ring road, I was relegated to the wake of two experienced riders enjoying an early morning side-by-side chat at better than twenty-five miles per hour. My humility was once again restored.

I had no doubt of his intent to use me as today's contribution to his bicycling ego.

The Ring Road has been a popular destination for Buffalonians for over 130 years.

18

My Laugh-In *Moment*

Lore has it that every new bicyclist with clipless pedals has a *Laugh-In* experience. One memorable, oft-repeated scene in Dan Rowan and Dick Martin's weekly sixty minutes of silly psychedelic humor was the full-grown man, Arte Johnson, wearing a rain slicker with a matching hat riding in sped-up motion on a child's tricycle. The five-second scene invariably ended with the mad tricyclist stopping abruptly, then tipping over sideways.

My *Laugh-In* moment came as I was leaving Delaware Park after a short ride one evening after work. Whether I was still thinking about work or was just seized by a momentary lapse of coordination, I failed to extricate my feet from the pedals when I stopped at the traffic light on Parkside Avenue.

Paralyzed and panicked, I tilted left and timbered to the pavement like a tree dropping under a woodsman's ax. The windows of the family van that I had barely missed opened slowly. I lay in the street attached helplessly to my $1,500 bike, looking up at two small boys with their heads out the windows snickering uncontrollably at my *Laugh-In* reprisal. My humility was once again restored.

Photo by Mary Gisel

Paralyzed and panicked,

I tilted left and timbered

to the pavement like a tree

dropping under

a woodsman's ax.

Ready to Go

19

Long Good-byes

Two weeks before our departure for Alaska, the final newsletter arrived from Pallotta. It brought good news in a short article titled "The Taper-Off." I raced to a phone to tell Ted that we were being officially instructed by the ride expert not to do any more hard rides. The taper-off days would allow us to rest and heal fully.

In those final two weeks, I rebuked with pleasure the subconscious voice in my head that had been harping "ride, ride, ride some more" for the past three months. I tried to relax, but ominous thoughts of the trial ahead stirred an adrenaline-fueled edginess most of my waking hours.

Aside from a brief mishap with UPS that threatened to send my bike to Albania instead of Alaska, the final ten days passed without incident. As we approached our August 18 departure date, I was amazed by the number of calls and visits I received from well wishers. As the frequency increased, I started to notice a pattern. Not one of these salutations would fit into the category of "Go get 'em, Tiger! You're going to conquer that route like Hannibal coming across the Himalayas." Rather, all but a few fell in the context of "I'm not sure what possessed you two to do this, but do your best to avoid being trampled, eaten, or frozen on this mindless odyssey." Most often these comments were in the form of "Have a great time, and be careful," with a heavy emphasis on the latter.

While I still appreciated the attention and well wishes, I was starting to wonder if these people somehow knew more than I did about the inherent dangers that lay ahead. I was starting to feel more like a newly minted first lieutenant heading to the front lines than a weekend sports enthusiast leaving on a pleasant bicycle trip.

My sister Barbara with Mary Rockwell and Ted in Lorraine Bay, Ontario, where our families reside in the summer.

This treatment was capped by a small send-off party at Mary and Rocky Rockwell's house near our summer residence in Canada two days before departure. While the thirty or so guests downed cases of Canadian lagers along with several half gallons of wine, Ted and I sipped on water as part of our pretrip hydration program. It was a good time with very good friends and family, including my mother, my sister Barbara, and, of course, Mary.

In addition to a few gag gifts and some highly entertaining old photos of Ted and me on our bikes as toddlers, several friends made short speeches, mostly humorous at our expense but in every case concluding with a serious toast to our success.

Mary, my mother, my sister Sally, and Ted celebrating the centennial of the
Pan-American Exposition before our departure for Alaska.

I was starting to feel more like a newly minted first lieutenant heading to the front lines than a weekend sports enthusiast leaving on a pleasant bicycle trip.

I enjoyed being the center of attention, but after a while I began to feel sheepish about being acclaimed for a feat I had not yet undertaken. What if I don't make it all the way? Would good social protocol suggest that I return the joke gifts and pay for all the water I drank?

20

Departure

Packing for travel, business or otherwise, ranks high on my list of least favorite activities. In my relentless drive to economize, I carefully evaluate the necessity of every individual item. I know this obsession is out of control when I find myself making special trips to CVS for that ultrasmall can of shaving cream. "Anything to save room" is my packing mantra.

The unfamiliar and unpredictable environment of Alaska presented a greater-than-usual packing challenge. Add in the trip complexities of multiple latitudes (north and south) and multiple altitudes (mountains and valleys) and I was all but undone.

On the eve of our departure, I stood in the center of our dining room, which I had appropriated in June as a staging area for my growing stash of new gear. This normally traditional dining room, with its gleaming hardwood floors, mahogany wainscoting, and antique table, now more closely resembled a bike shop liquidation sale.

Our house, even with two grammar school–age children, was always clean and orderly. For Mary, a magazine left on the floor of the den is like fingernails scraping across a chalkboard. As she moves from room to room, her radar detects any out-of-place items. Working her hands with grace and efficiency, she accumulates all the offending clothes, books, dishware, and sports equipment, leaving in her wake the orderliness of a neat but comfortable home. Her silent acceptance of my abuse of our dining room was another testament to Mary's emotional support of my adventure.

In addition to spare pedals, bike tubes, energy bars, first-aid kits, bike bags, flashlights, bug repellent, and other paraphernalia, small piles of clothes—from hats to shoes and everything in between—were positioned randomly on the floor and antique table. "Gore-tex," "microfleece," "synthetic," and other marvels of apparel chemistry promised to keep me dry and reasonably warm regardless of rain from the outside or perspiration from within.

In the center of the scene was the single green duffel bag into which all of my belongings would have to fit. Once the sleeping bag went in, there was about a shopping bag's volume of space left for the rest of the clothes and gear. Three hours and four repackings later, I closed up the bag for the final time, still doubting if I had included the right mix of gear.

The next morning, Ted and Ginna arrived to give me a ride to the airport. Mary, Hanna, and Will all came outside for a final farewell and, of course, one last plea from Mary that we be careful.

As we cruised east along the open expressway, I contemplated that I had never been out of touch with my family for more than a day or two. On this trip, I would not be able to talk to them for six days. This thought added sadness to my current emotional blend of anxiety and excitement. I pushed back against these welling emotions with a self-declaration that I would never be more ready for this challenge than I was on that day. The notion that my next pedal stroke would be "real" and no longer "practice" was a source of relief and energy.

Our Northwest Airlines route to Fairbanks went via Detroit and then six hours to Anchorage. Ted and I settled into our familiar bike conversation about the steepness of hills, average speeds, and flat tires. We also continued our hydration program, each slugging down a half dozen glasses of water until the flight attendant informed us that, due to Northwest's fifty-million-dollar loss the previous quarter, there was a cutback on bottled water.

As our fellow passengers were more interested in scotch and wine, we managed to horde most of the water inventory for ourselves. Between us, we made nine trips to the bathroom during the six hours. After each of us had made our third trip, the woman seated behind us started to watch us a little more carefully, no doubt searching our faces for telltale signs of drug use or other deviant behavior.

Arriving on schedule in Anchorage, we navigated our way to the Alaska Air flight that would take us to Fairbanks. As we approached the gate area, it was evident that many of our fellow travelers were also on the bike trip. I couldn't help eyeing them to gauge their ages and fitness levels. To my dismay, they looked to be in their twenties, athletic, and casually confident.

The few travelers my age were clinging to Orvis fly-rod cases, no doubt recently purchased in anticipation of some corporate-sponsored fishing trip to Alaska. Relaxed in their casual but expensive khakis, they laughed and sipped beers as they waited for the flight to board. I wondered how I had ended up on the bike ride instead of the fishing trip, which was sure to incorporate the comforts of home within the Alaska wilderness.

It was midafternoon as the plane headed north to Fairbanks. In these northern latitudes of Alaska, the sun still shone high in the sky. The mammoth glaciers near Anchorage gave way briefly to the Susitna River Valley,

Harry Walker/PictureQuest

and soon we approached the Alaska Range. The partially clear skies gave us full view of the range's most striking sight, Mt. McKinley.

Rising over twenty thousand feet out of the rugged terrain, McKinley, also known as "Denali" by native Alaskans, is the highest peak in North America. The absence of any civilization in the surrounding Denali National Park added to the purity of the view. I was humbled by the thought that this sight, untouched by man, had changed very little in thousands of years.

I considered the irony that a natural wonder of such enduring memory should be named after a president who is known for accomplishing so little during his term in office. The irony was heightened by the fact that President McKinley was assassinated in Buffalo exactly one hundred years before, in 1901. As the mountain passed below us, I resolved to refer to it in the future only as Denali, a name that more fittingly echoed the grandeur of this snow-capped peak.

Continuing toward Fairbanks, there was no letdown in the scenery of Alaska's interior. While part of the United States, Alaska has little in common with the rest of the country. The combination of its sparse population and its extraordinary expansiveness sets it apart. A mere 626,000 Alaskans inhabit an area of more than 590,000 square miles. This area constitutes more than one-fifth of our entire country. At approximately one square mile per person, it's the equivalent of seven people inhabiting

I wondered how I had ended up on the bike ride instead of the fishing trip, which was sure to incorporate the comforts of home.

all of Manhattan. With about half of the Alaskans concentrated in the coastal city of Anchorage, there are broad interior regions that remain uninhabited and almost inaccessible.

The state is aptly known by the natives as "Alyeska," which translates to "the land of the great." Spreading out across the arctic north portion of the globe, Alaska includes the northernmost, easternmost, and westernmost parts of the United States. It contains seventy active volcanoes, over one hundred thousand glaciers, and seventeen of the twenty highest peaks in the nation. We would have the privilege over the next few days of passing through some of these regions. First, however, we would spend a day and a half in Fairbanks preparing for our departure.

The state is aptly known by the natives as "Alyeska" which translates to "the land of the great." Spreading out across the arctic north portion of the globe, Alaska includes the northernmost, easternmost, and western-most parts of the United States. It contains seventy active volcanoes, over one hundred thousand glaciers and seventeen of the twenty highest peaks in the nation.

21

Fairbanks

The city of Fairbanks is a study in contrasts. It seems insignificant and lost amid the scale of Alaska's interior. Scattered haphazardly on both banks of the Chena River, Fairbanks's featureless buildings look worn and tired. Their gloomy appearance speaks to the struggles of the city's residents to sustain themselves over the century since Fairbanks was founded.

Over the past hundred years, external forces have pushed and pulled the fates of Fairbanks. Boom times filled with optimism have been followed by periods of near extinction. Like its extreme swings in temperature, from a high of 99° Fahrenheit to a low of −66° Fahrenheit, Fairbanks has exhibited scant control over its fortunes.

Even its location was an accident. In 1901, Captain E. T. Barnette was on his way to establish a trading post

on the Valdez-Eagle trail where it crossed the Tanana River. Detoured by shallow water, his trip ended on the banks of the Chena River seven miles shy of its intersection with the Tanana. Barnette never fulfilled his plan to move his goods to the intended site. He started supplying a few prospectors from this accidental location and soon named the new settlement after Charles Fairbanks, a senator from Indiana.

In the ensuing years, Fairbanks enjoyed peaks of temporary prosperity driven by the discovery of gold, the military buildups during World War II and later the cold war, the discovery of oil, and the building of the Alaska pipeline project. Between these up periods were equally sharp troughs, including the devastating effects of floods and fires, as well as poverty, unemployment, and starvation during recessionary times. The military spending included the construction of the Trans-Alaska highway, upon which our AIDS Vaccine Ride would commence.

After settling into our hotel, Ted and I set out on foot to see the city and find some dinner. After enjoying a plate of pasta in a quaint, crowded restaurant, we decided to explore. The treeless, flat riverbanks upon which Fairbanks was built made it easy for us to spot the older part of town, near the bridge crossing the Chena River. A visitor's center provided some historical highlights of the major happenings in Fairbanks history, while choosing to omit any references to the decades of despair.

As if to fill in these historical omissions, a collection of impoverished native Alaskans loitered in the courtyard outside the center. A few were drunk and protesting loudly as one of their group was being led away in handcuffs by the local police. His head

pitched forward, his long, matted hair hid his face as he staggered helplessly toward the patrol car.

It was not the mythical first impression of Alaska that we had anticipated. We were reminded that Alaska is not a wilderness theme park but a harsh environment that has posed extraordinary physical, social, and economic challenges to its inhabitants since humans first journeyed across the land bridge.

The native Alaskans whom we encountered were of Athabaskan descent, one of several distinct groups of natives who still make up a significant percentage of the state's population. The Athabaskans occupied the interior regions, while the Tlingit lived along the more temperate southern coast, and the Aleuts were from the peninsula and the Aleutian islands. Finally, among all the native Alaskans, the Yupik and Inupiaq Eskimos have survived the harshest conditions, living well above the Arctic Circle on Alaska's shores of the Arctic Ocean.

The first colonists did not arrive in the region until the Russians ventured by ship to the outer Aleutians around 1740. Further exploration and settlement by the Russians, Europeans, and Americans progressed slowly and was driven only by the fur trade and the abundance of sea otters off the Aleutians. In 1867, the United States purchased the territory from Russia for $7.2 million (about two cents an acre). Just thirty-five years later, the discovery of gold prompted an onslaught of new settlers. After gold, it was oil that brought more outsiders. As elsewhere in the world, the natives were brutally abused and oppressed by these newcomers. As Ted and I witnessed in Fairbanks, the scars from this treatment are evident today in the poverty and indigence of the native population.

The city of Fairbanks is a study in contrasts.

67

22

Paul and Bushy

Paul Nelson and Ted Inbusch.

During our three months of training, Ted and I were consoled in the knowledge that we would be joined on the ride by two other Williams College friends, Paul Nelson and Ted Inbusch. It was Ted Inbusch (a.k.a. "Bushy") who prompted our participation after seeing an ad in a bike magazine more than a year before. His call to Ted Walsh prompted Ted's call to me and the rest is—well, you know. Since the sleeping accommodations on the ride were two-person tents, and none of us was too excited about bunking with a random stranger, there was considerable focus on attracting a fourth member to the team. We were successful in late May, when Paul Nelson signed on after being heavily recruited by Bushy at their twenty-fifth Williams reunion.

Among the four of us, Bushy was the only one with previous experience, having worked in a bike shop during one summer vacation a few decades ago. After graduating from Williams, he embarked on a Wall Street financial career for a few years before joining Borden. As a financial executive, he moved through several parts of the Borden organization, including a five-year stint in Sao Paolo, Brazil. Like many other public corporations, Borden has gone through some major restructuring and divestitures in recent years, prompting Bushy to depart just a couple months before our ride.

His last assignment was in Columbus, Ohio, where he still lives today with his wife, Catherine, and their three children. While conveniently unemployed during the training months, Bushy successfully resumed his job search after returning from the ride.

Having arrived in Fairbanks just before midnight, Bushy and Paul agreed to meet Ted and me the next morning in the hotel coffee shop. Aside from a few gray hairs, Bushy looked unchanged from the last time I saw him in 1975. His personality was also unaffected by the transition through adulthood, career, and family. He was a pure extrovert who engages unabashedly anyone and anything he encountered. Like Chevy Chase, his boyish good looks masked an impish wry humor. The combination could be disconcerting, particularly for first-time encounters. With over one thousand new people to meet over the coming week, Bushy was as excited as a ten-year-old at the gates of Disney.

True to his abundant enthusiasm, he had purchased matching team bike jerseys for the four of us. They were black and personalized respectively with our name in yellow lettering on the front. In Bushy's perpetual lighthearted style, he also had inscribed "Team Ted" on the left sleeve of each jersey. It was his way of subtly poking fun both at us and at the numerous more serious bicycling teams who were attending the Alaska ride. Of course, Ted, Paul, and I loved this sartorial sarcasm, and we frequently paraded around together wearing our team shirts during the course of the week.

Our parade started that Sunday, the hectic day of preparation and registration before the beginning of the ride. This was Day Zero, when eleven hundred riders all crammed into the Carlson Center, the small Fairbanks

arena that is home to local hockey and basketball teams and assorted conventions.

In addition to registration, Day Zero is designed to bring the riders together both physically and spiritually before taking on the grueling task ahead. The collective enthusiasm and anxiety created a collegial atmosphere where strangers greeted each other with none of their ordinary inhibitions.

Of course, this was standard behavior for Bushy, who

Team Ted.

breezed through the crowd like a presidential candidate. In one of his dozens of encounters, a woman excitedly quizzed Bushy about his hometown and the other usual banter before noticing the inscription on his sleeve. Assuming of course that there was a deep, meaningful story behind the name (such as riding in honor of a relative or friend who had been stricken with AIDS), the woman

Like Chevy Chase,

his boyish good looks masked

an impish wry humor.

Among the four of us, Bushy was the only one with previous experience, having worked in a bike shop during one summer vacation a few decades ago. . . .

Paul is a true Renaissance man. While earning his living with his creativity and hand skills, he also has an endless curiosity and quest for knowledge in all subjects.

turned serious and respectfully asked, "So, please tell me all about Team Ted!"

Bushy's deadpan response was "My name is Ted."

The tone of his voice suggested that this fact should have been obvious to the now-perplexed woman. Her expression darkened and with an emphatic disdain, she blurted back, "So it's all about you?"

Bushy joyfully assumed the role of the self-centered athlete and played it to perfection until the woman turned away in utter disgust. Without another thought, he also moved on, eagerly seeking his next encounter.

Paul Nelson took the less traveled road when he graduated from Williams. While a majority of his classmates headed off to careers in law, banking, medicine, and education, Paul became a shipbuilder. After building sailboats on both the Atlantic and Pacific coasts, he returned to his native Massachusetts to build custom homes. Tiring of the endless pursuit of reliable employees, he "downsized" a few years ago to a one-man operation, building high-quality, handcrafted custom furniture.

Paul was a true Renaissance man. While earning his living with his creativity and hand skills, he also had an endless curiosity and quest for knowledge in all subjects. His unpretentious self-deprecating demeanor masked an enviable intellect and a light-speed wit. With his nonstop banter and command of various New England dialects, Paul was a continuous source of entertainment and laughter. Paul lived outside Boston with his wife, Debbie, and their two boys.

For Bushy the Alaska trip was a smorgasbord of new people to engage. For Paul the trip was a vast new territory to explore and discover. Like me, Paul was caught up in the challenge to research and master the many nuances of a new sport. Finally, Ted combined elements of each of us and in so doing quickly brought us together.

After only moments of our breakfast reunion at the hotel on Day Zero, Team Ted was born.

Bushy, Ted, Paul, and me.

The Ride

23

Pallotta TeamWorks and Day Zero

Pallotta TeamWorks was the nonprofit promoter of the Alaska AIDS Vaccine Ride. Founded in 1992, Pallotta's inaugural event was the California AIDS Ride, a seven-day ride from San Francisco to Los Angeles. It was originated by Dan Pallotta, who remained the founder, owner, and CEO of Pallotta TeamWorks until the final event concluded in 2002.

A 1983 Harvard graduate and a fierce social activist, Dan Pallotta had already organized major events relating to world hunger and global disarmament before turning his attention to AIDS and breast cancer. In its decade of existence, Pallotta Team-Works raised over $300 million for AIDS- and breast cancer–related charities. In so doing, the organization brought over three million new donors to the causes of AIDS and breast cancer.

Ted in the Carlson Center on Day Zero.

Pallotta TeamWorks claimed to be "America's premier producer of human potential events." This public relations tag line revealed its uniqueness and the foundation for its success. Each event offered participants the combination of raising funds for a worthy cause and taking on a life-altering personal experience. It's a bit like United Way meets Outward Bound. The blend was highly alluring and effective. In both fund-raising and training, partici-

pants have the dual motivation of personal achievement and simply "doing good." Each individual's motivational mix may be weighted differently, but for Pallotta the results were the same—energized people raising millions of dollars to fight life-threatening diseases.

Through several years of increasing success and learning, Pallotta had finely tuned its events. Interestingly, Pallotta focused on the same two elements that have also been the secret of the Wal-Mart success in mass retailing—logistics and spirit.

While Wal-Mart has excelled at managing its vast supply chain of goods, Pallotta mastered the science of managing a "people supply chain." Consider the logistics required to account and care for over eleven hundred individual bike riders and another one thousand volunteer crew members as they make their way across the barren terrain of Alaska. Each participant arrived with a bicycle (often in several pieces), a single duffel bag, and an abundance of anxiety. From there the Pallotta logistical machine took over.

Volunteer crew members had arrived one day earlier to be trained and assigned to various duties, ranging from truck driver to lunch server. As the riders arrived at the Carlson Center on Day Zero, they were processed in batches through a sequence of stations to register, be assigned a tent number, verify fund-raising goals, and confirm health information.

During the course of the six-day ride, the Pallotta machine was calibrated to stay one step ahead of us riders. Pit stops, lunch stops, and camps were erected and dismantled each day with the military precision of an army advancing doggedly into enemy territory. Each day was unique in the terrain we faced but was routine in the orderly repetition of our movements. We ate, drank, and rode our way to camp, where we pitched tents, showered, ate, and slept. The routine was set and was essential to keep this "bicycle army" moving safely across the unforgiving landscape. We pedaled as individuals, but otherwise we were cogs in the Pallotta machine.

Like Wal-Mart, Pallotta developed a superior capability in logistics. But both organizations' performances have also been fueled by a second shared trait: the ability to move the spirit. Much of Wal-Mart's success can be traced to the collective spirit and attitude of its employees (known as "associates"). They are the product of a culture derived from the down-home, hard-working, people-friendly values of Wal-Mart's founder, Sam Walton.

Such is the case with Pallotta Team-Works. The culture and environment of each event were laced with Dan Pallotta's values of "individually stretching oneself to achieve more than one thought possible" and "people of all origins coming together to make an impact on the world we live in."

The final stop in the Day Zero sequence of registration was the safety briefing. Though the advance communi-cations from Pallotta were laden with emphatic discussions about safety priorities and policies, the Day Zero video effectively drove home the risks we would face in the coming days. The message was not new, but the stark prediction that "someone will die if you fail to stay alert" added an unneeded edge to our existing anxiety.

The safety message was poignant, but the rest of the briefing was even more influential. It was ten minutes of Dan Pallotta sharing his vision of the world as a better place through the actions of individuals like us seeking to make a difference. He encouraged us to start the week by changing our attitudes and behavior to elevate the levels of compassion and consideration for those around us. We each could make a conscious decision to act with kindness, a behavior summed up in the Dan Pallotta's parlance as "humankind."

It was a compelling message delivered with passion and sincerity. Before our feet touched the pedals for the first rotation, a shared spirit drew the participants together. We had accomplished nothing yet, but we felt good about ourselves.

Before our feet touched the pedals for the first rotation, a shared spirit drew the participants together.

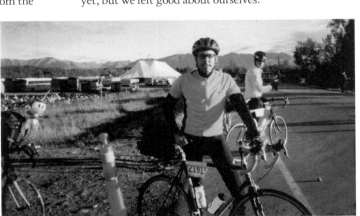

Ready to go.

24
Day One

I didn't need the 4:30 a.m. wake-up call on Day One. The four-hour time difference combined with nervous anticipation had me up and in the shower by 4 o'clock. Emerging from our hotel an hour later, the four members of Team Ted eased willingly into the waiting arms of Pallotta's logisitics. A small bus was there to take us and one of the volunteer crew members to the Carlson Center for yoga stretching, a breakfast of fruit and granola bars, and the official start.

As an antidote to our quiet nervousness, Ted stoked up a polite conversation on the bus with the crew mem-

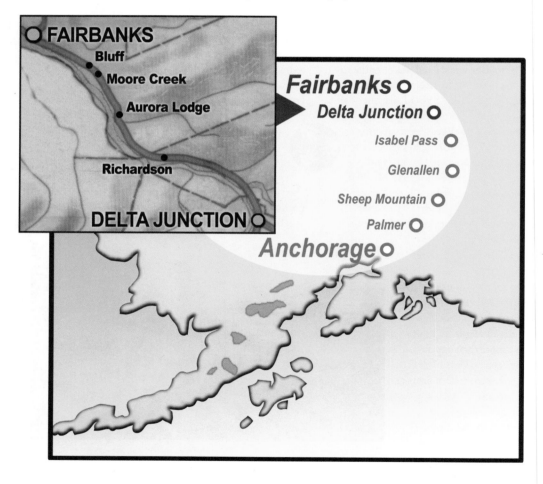

ber named John. We were all perplexed by the willingness of these crew members to pay their own way to Alaska, where they would spend twelve hours a day performing menial tasks in the service of strangers on bicycles. John, we learned, was actually there to support his wife, who had been training to ride in this event for over a year.

Three days later, I bumped into John in camp and asked him how his wife was doing. He responded, "Not so good. She made it to the seventy-mile mark on Day One and had to quit and take the van the rest of the way." He added that she was sobbing as she emerged from the van. Her yearlong goal was to ride the whole way, and she was defeated on the first day.

The opening ceremony, conducted in the darkened arena, was a well-scripted production. The pounding background music bore a close resemblance to the *Rocky* theme song. The voiceover comments revisited the Pallotta values and praised the participants for their strength and conviction. By the end of the thirty-minute program, the entire arena was pulsing with energy and anticipation.

As we made our way outside to find our bikes, I was momentarily struck with amazement that I was actually going to do this—*right now*. The crowd moved slowly at first, and we had to walk our bikes for the first couple hundred yards. Leaving no detail overlooked, Pallotta arranged for an Athabaskan chief to chant a blessing for a safe ride. He wafted smoke through our ranks as we edged past the starting line. The red Alaska sun was creeping over the horizon as the crowd stretched out and we were finally able to start pedaling.

Day One was just shy of one hundred miles. The route took us southeast out of Fairbanks on the Richardson Highway. The road was constructed along the north bank of the Tanana River, which we would follow throughout the day.

Rivers in Alaska look different. The permafrost beneath the river beds prevents them from carving deep, defined routes. As a result, when water levels rise, they expand laterally in a floodlike manner, creating a tangled web of individual flows carrying the chalky silt across the landscape.

We made our first stop of the day at a predetermined outpost about twenty miles from the start in the small town of North Pole, Alaska. Aside from a handful of rundown shops clustered along the side of the Richardson Highway, the town boasted a forty-foot-high wooden sculpture of Santa Claus standing at the edge of the dirt parking lot that serviced the shops. A number of riders succumbed to their tourist instincts and lined up to have their pictures taken in front of the hulking Santa. I considered the sculpture a minor man-made blemish on the pristine face of Alaska's natural environment, so I turned my attention to the offerings of our first outpost of Day One.

Teams of nonriding volunteers had set up a dozen folding tables in a U shape.  The bottom of the U was laden with a variety of snacks, including granola bars, pretzels, and fruit. At a few outposts, including this one, volunteers prepared mini open-faced bagel sandwiches spread with peanut butter and topped with bananas and raisins. The right side of the U was reserved for bever-

As we made our way outside to find our bikes, I was momentarily struck with amazement that I was actually going to do this— right now.

Ted and Paul following our lunch break atop the banks of the Tanana River.

ages, usually a line of coolers dispensing sports drinks and water.

Even if we did not feel hungry or thirsty, we were encouraged to eat and drink at every outpost. We recognized without question the importance of being hydrated, but eating frequently was equally critical. In my preride training research, I discovered that different physiologists and sports trainers offer a variety of theories on the optimum selection and mix of food consumption to support endurance training. The common accepted premise is that we burn calories through all physical activity. In a normal day, someone of my size (about 170 pounds) would use about fifteen hundred calories. However, on our Day One ride, I would burn more than seven thousand calories.*

A majority of caloric intake should come from carbohydrates, which our bodies convert to glycogen. Glycogen, the primary source of energy, is stored in the muscles and becomes depleted after short stints of exercise. Without refueling, you quickly become dizzy and tired, a phenomenon known in Bicyclese as "bonking."

In my preride training, I had suffered the experience of bonking during one long ride when I neglected to bring along enough food. My leg muscles were reduced

*Ed Burke, *Cycling Health and Physiology*, 2nd ed., p. 100.

to wet noodles, and each pedal stroke sapped my entire body. After limping the last few miles to my parked car, I had to lie down on the grass for ten minutes before I could muster the energy to put my bike on the rack. This valuable lesson stayed with me throughout the ride, and I never bypassed the abundant food table at the outposts.

The other side of the U-shaped tables was reserved for minor medical remedies—Advil for aching muscles, bandages and gauze for cuts, and various remedies for saddle sores. The latter result from the continuous repetitive friction between the seat and the rider's inner thigh or crotch area. *Saddle sore* is an all-purpose term for maladies ranging from minor chafing to infected skin ulcers.* Even the less serious variety can turn an enjoyable ride into a miserable existence with each pedal stroke, unleashing a branding iron sensation to the crotch. My preride anxieties had included a healthy paranoia about saddle sores, and I came equipped with my personal jar of chamois cream. I need not have bothered since there was ample supply of this Criscolike, petroleum-based cream at every outpost. It was not unusual to witness half a dozen riders scooping a fistful of the salve and reaching down the front of their bicycle pants to spread the soothing goo across the afflicted areas.

Team Ted did not dwell long at this first outpost. We still had more than eighty miles to cover and were not sure how our conditioning would hold up to the road ahead. After refueling our energy stores and refilling our water bottles, we were back on our bikes, heading out of North Pole, Alaska, even as many other riders were just arriving. Our first stop behind us, the ride started to

develop a comfortable rhythm. Fewer bikes passed others on Day One than on any other day. Since all of the participants started at about the same time, their abilities and speeds sorted the thousand men and women into like groupings, with the fastest riders out front and the slowest in the rear.

With little need to focus on passing, we were free to absorb sights of the Alaska plains and the slow-moving, glacier-fed river. Just as the landscape helped ward off the monotony of the long flat ride, I also stayed busy talking with Bushy, Ted, and Paul. On some stretches, the highway shoulder widened enough to enable two of us to ride side by side, a practice that violated one of the safety rules but that we indulged in nonetheless.

I frequently checked my bike computer, gauging our speed and calculating distance to the next stop. With the aid of the computer, I was able to keep the challenging ride in perspective. Rather than feeling oppressed or anxious about the long distances yet to travel, the computer allowed me to chunk the ride into more manageable mileages. There are many analogous philosophies in sports and life, all built around a theme of focusing on the current task and letting the long term take care of itself. A house builder lays one brick at a time, a professional golfer succeeds by concentrating on hitting each individual shot, and the bicyclist's unit of measure is each pedal stroke or revolution.

Through my training, I learned that I achieved optimum efficiency when I was pedaling between eighty-five and ninety revolutions per minute. At this level I could maintain the maximum speed without exhausting myself. My computer fed me information on my RPMs, enabling me to stay in my optimum range with the use of my twenty-one different gears. Riding along on Day One, I calculated in my head that traveling the

*Fred Mathey, "Saddle Sores: Banish Them Forever," in *"Bicycling Magazine's" Complete Books of Road Cycling Skills*, ed. Ed Pavelka, p. 164).

Our first stop behind us, the ride started to develop a comfortable rhythm.

An arching rainbow provided a soulful backdrop to our Day One campsite at Delta Junction.

entire five hundred miles would require approximately two hundred thousand pedal strokes, many on long, uphill stretches I had yet to encounter.

A few hours out, we left behind the flat plains that are home to Fairbanks. The soaring peaks of the Alaska Range came into distant view, and we started to gently climb. It was sunny and seventy degrees. As we left the last bits of Fairbanks civilization behind, four F-18 fighter jets from Wainwright Air Force Base roared overhead and saluted us with a "wing wag." I watched them as long as I could until they banked to the east and folded into the skyscape. The natural quiet of the wilderness returned. I smiled at the pleasure of being part of this moment and picked up my pace.

Ted, Bushy, Paul, and I arrived in camp about 4 p.m., having climbed about a thousand feet in elevation and feeling pretty strong. Our confidence ran high. We knew there would be tougher climbs ahead but sensed we were well prepared.

That was not the case with many other riders. Later that evening, around 8 a.m., we were still lingering in the dinner tent when an official announced that the final rider was just about to enter camp. Hundreds of us streamed across the field to the camp entrance to cheer this very tired man who struggled alone across the final few yards of the day. It took him fourteen hours, but somehow he avoided being swept up by the "sag vans" patrolling the route to pick up stragglers. Judging from his rusty bike, wide tires, and wind jacket, he was not a serious bicyclist. It was then that I sensed that many of the other participants had a variety of different perspectives on the ride.

Three distinct groups came together to participate in the Alaska AIDS Vaccine Ride. The first consisted of the "bikers." Mostly in their twenties, this group's primary focus was on the biking experience, the challenge to conquer this daunting five-hundred-mile trek across Alaska. They came equipped with the sleekest road bikes from Trek, Bianchi, and Canondale and were adorned with the latest bike-wear fashions. This was their arena, and they strutted confidently through the opening day crowd, festooned in their colors, like the jockeys at the starting gate of the Kentucky Derby.

The next group comprised the gay participants. Many of these riders and crew members had participated in ten or more previous Pallotta events. While the vast majority of AIDS sufferers around the world are not homosexuals, that is not the case in the United States, where most AIDS victims are gay. The impact of the disease on the gay community has been profound, and Dan Pallotta's efforts to fight back was appealing to many of that community. They were in Alaska primarily to support the cause. Included in their ranks were a number of HIV-positive men and women whose courage was highlighted throughout the week.

The last major group of participants were riding in honor of someone close who had succumbed to this terrible disease. At dinner one night, I sat behind a husband and wife who appeared to be in their early fifties. They each wore a T-shirt silk-screened with a photo of their son who had died in 2000 at the age of twenty-four. Coming to Alaska was part of their grieving process, and they were not alone. At each camp, a small "bereavement tent" was set up where family and friends of AIDS victims could sit quietly and pray or reflect. The quiet suffering of these people was powerful. I will not forget the face of the young man on the T-shirt. That, I'm sure, was his parents' intent.

Of course, not all eleven hundred riders fit perfectly into this description. Ted, Bushy, Paul, and I mostly resembled the "serious bikers," except for our ages and our beyond-conservative black attire. Certainly, we were there primarily for the adventure, but we all conceded that the cause enhanced our motivation as the event progressed.

Others we met also escaped easy classification in one of these three groups. On the third day, we were joined at lunch by Paula, a thirty-something schoolteacher from Portland. She had signed up after reading an article about the rapid spread of the AIDS virus. She realized that statistically about a quarter of her seventh grade students were likely to be infected. She knew she "had to do something," so she signed up to do the ride.

This unusual panoply of people with diverse motivations and origins descended on Alaska with a single purpose but left with far more than the gratification that comes from an athletic challenge. Many found peace, some found courage, but we all came away with a new level of enlightenment.

I will not forget the face of the young man on the T-shirt. That, I'm sure, was his parents' intent.

25

Day Two

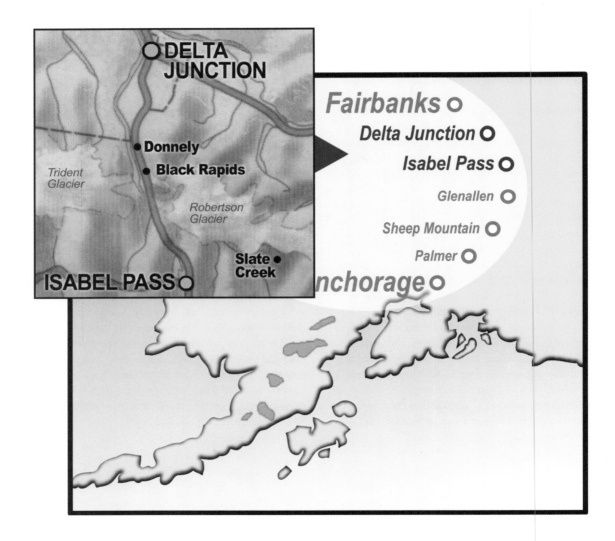

Each day of the ride quickly developed a familiar routine—get up, eat breakfast, pack our bags and tents, ride all day to the next camp, pitch tents, shower, eat dinner, and go to bed.

Early each morning, I would thrash about in the cramped confines of our small tent to pull on clothes within my reach. After invariably stepping on Ted in my vain attempt to exit the tent gracefully, I'd amble over to the food tent to get coffee and copies of *The VacScene*. This one-sheet newsletter was billed as "The Daily Journal of the Pallotta TeamWorks AIDS Vaccine Ride."

After taking my first sip of coffee to warm my insides, I scanned *The VacScene* in search of the description of that day's ride, complete with mileage, scenic features, and the route elevation map. The latter showed the various ups and downs that we would be facing during the course of the day as well as the placement of four outposts along the way. In bold letters below the elevation map was the warning (repeated every day)—"If you don't reach an outpost by its closing time, you will have to board a bus and be taken to camp."

Our preride manual elaborated that any rider who refused to board a bus after falling behind schedule would be immediately ejected from the event. The message was simple: "Keep up, or else." Many participants were forced to board the buses every day. For Ted, Bushy, Paul, and me, taking the bus would amount to failure. We were there to ride every foot of every mile.

In addition to other bits of information, each *VacScene* also included a cover story about one of the participants. The cover story on Day Two introduced Steve Case; his wife, Carter, and their two children, Scott and Ann. We first met Scott on Day Zero when he noticed Paul wearing shorts with a logo from Williams College. There is a special bond among Williams alumni, and Scott, a recent graduate, stopped to chat with Paul. We saw him again that evening at the salmon-bake dinner in Fairbanks and had the opportunity there to meet the rest of the family.

Having just completed running the Boston Marathon, Scott was not in Alaska to ride but rather join his mother and sister as crew members in support of their father.

Scott's father, Steve Case, was a white, middle-class heterosexual man married for thirty-five years. He was also HIV positive. He contracted the virus when he was accidentally stabbed with a used needle two years earlier in a crowded mall in Vancouver. While the family could have kept Steve's HIV status a secret, they decided to go public and deal openly with the stigma attached to the disease. Steve and Carter have shared their story, educated others, and even traveled to South Africa in their work to support AIDS relief groups.

We saw Steve and his family frequently through the week, and you would never know he was HIV positive. He was always smiling, talking, and anxious to tackle the next incline. Although a few years older, Steve was much like us. The only difference was that he carried the virus. We were impressed by his courage and his character.

Scott, as it turned out, was just one of a dozen Williams alumni on the trip. Through the camp grapevine, we tracked them all down and staged a Williams College picture on the fourth evening. The Williams riders were predominantly members of the "serious bikers" group. They were athletic adventure seekers who had graduated within the last couple years.

Scott Case, second from right, with the other fellow Williams College alumni on the ride.

I was the ranking alumnus among the group and shocked some of them, and myself, with the observation that I had graduated from Williams before a few of them had been born.

The Day Two ride was only seventy-five miles but was all uphill. As we departed camp, we passed the intersection with the Alaska Highway. Built by the military during World War II, this two-lane road was the first physical connection between the Alaska territory and the United States. It was viewed as a critical strategic access to Alaska where the United States had built substantial military infrastructure in defense of a possible invasion from Asia.

Passing the terminus of the Alaska Highway, we continued on the Richardson Highway and headed into the Alaska Mountain Range. Our camp destination was a place nicknamed "Top of the World" at Isabel Pass.

Unlike Day One, riders on Day Two and the other four days were free to start at anytime, the only caution being the need to reach each outpost of the day's route prior to its closing. We tended to start each day near the middle of the pack, but our pace was faster than the average rider, especially on the uphill segments. On a long, grueling ride, it is disheartening and debilitating to lose your rhythmic momentum for any reason. Being forced to decelerate for a log jam of slower riders ahead carries the same frustration as sitting in a traffic jam caused by a stalled car. You can see wide open spaces in the distance, but you just can't get there. Such was the case on Day Two as Paul and I came upon the longest uphill segment after lunch. Scores of riders were clustered in a tight line, inching their way up the hill like a line of ants crawling up a tree. The few who could not keep the pace had faltered and were on foot, trudging their bikes toward the crest. Their presence forced the line of slow riders to default out to the left edge of the shoulder, leaving no room on the shoulder for faster riders to pass by. The choice left to the faster riders was to fall in behind and accept the slower pace or venture onto the highway to execute passes. Among other traffic, the highway was home to an endless fleet of logging trucks, which hurtled by our left shoulders with little warning. While passing one rider at a time posed very little risk, we were now forced to consider the need to pass ten or even twenty riders before finding a gap in the line that would provide safe refuge.

Paul was in front of me as we approached the long hill, and he gave no indication he would fall in behind the slower moving line of riders. I stayed close to his rear wheel, and the two of us veered onto the highway and pushed up past the first dozen riders with little trouble. His confidence bolstered, Paul eased back onto the highway as we neared the next cluster of bikes. Having passed the first ten riders in this group, I looked up beyond Paul to see that we had at least twenty more to get past. My eyes dropped instinctively to my rearview mirror, where I saw two heavily loaded trucks just starting up the hill about a hundred yards behind us. The thick roar of their engines jumped an octave as the drivers downshifted to maintain

their momentum up the incline. I yelled, "Trucks behind!" at Paul's back, and I could see him lean forward in his saddle as he tried to increase speed. Accelerating significantly uphill is nearly impossible for anyone other than Lance Armstrong. It was apparent we could not reach the front of the line before the trucks reached us. The driver of the first truck leaned on his horn, further fueling my mounting panic. With the trucks twenty yards back and gaining, Paul spotted a small gap in the line, just enough for one bike. He veered back onto the shoulder and pushed as far right as possible so I could slide in by his side. The trucks charged past, giving no ground or hint of sympathy for our dilemma. I could have licked the right side mirror of the second truck had I been so inclined. With its trailing wind still in my face, I veered back onto the highway. Paul was coming up fast on two riders walking with their bikes up the right side of the shoulder. He slid into the void I had created and just brushed past the rear walker. Stabilizing his line, Paul glanced over at me, and we shared our unspoken admission of our good fortune.

While the route was unvaringly uphill, the weather was anything but consistent. Paul and I rode together for most of the day and stopped several times to don raingear and booties, black neoprene covers that slipped over our biking shoes. With our black booties and black tights we resembled oversized merry men in a bad school production of *Robin Hood*. But with a cold rain falling and three thousand feet of elevation to climb, we had long forsaken any concern for appearances.

We pushed ahead hard, passing dozens of riders stalled on the steeper inclines. We were pleased, and somewhat surprised, to finish among the first one hundred riders. We both acknowledged that our competitive juices were flowing, despite being continuously reminded by Pallotta officials that "it is not a race."

Our Day Two camp location was a rock plateau a few

With our black booties and black tights we resembled oversized merry men in a bad school production of Robin Hood.

Bushy and Ted starting to set up at Isabel Pass where the Gulkana Galcier forms an ominous backdrop for our campground.

miles below the Gulkana Glacier. With their spirits of adventure soaring, Ted and Bushy cajoled Paul and me to join them for a hike up to the glacier. I was reluctant at first because I knew we needed to rest, but we had plenty of daylight, and, as usual, Ted and Bushy were relentless. We were light-hearted and joking as we headed out on what appeared to be a short climb to the glacier's lower edge. Two hours later, we were less than halfway to the glacier, and our moods had darkened along with the sky. We made it to a wobbly suspension bridge spanning one of the mammoth glacier's multiple icy runoffs. After taking a few pictures, we turned back. We regretted stopping short of our destination, but our collective prudence prevailed as we contemplated the four remaining days of biking.

That evening as we sat in the food tent, the temperature plummeted, and the rain came down in sheets. Scores of riders abandoned their tents as the mountain winds separated rain flies from the tent tops. Our hike had been a reminder of the magnitude of the spaces in Alaska. Now we were being reminded of the unpredictable harsh environment in these mountains so near the Arctic Circle.

As we dashed back from the large dinner area, our tent looked smaller than usual and seemed like meager shelter from the fierce winds and driving rain. It was our only choice. There was nowhere else to go. Ted and I

crawled into our sleeping bags, wondering how much water the rocky ground would absorb before it started flowing into our tent. Being cold was a discomfort. The prospect of being cold and wet was a danger. The water was already dripping through the slanted ceiling on my side as I closed my eyes and tried to sleep.

Our Day Two hike to the glacier fell short.

26

Day Three

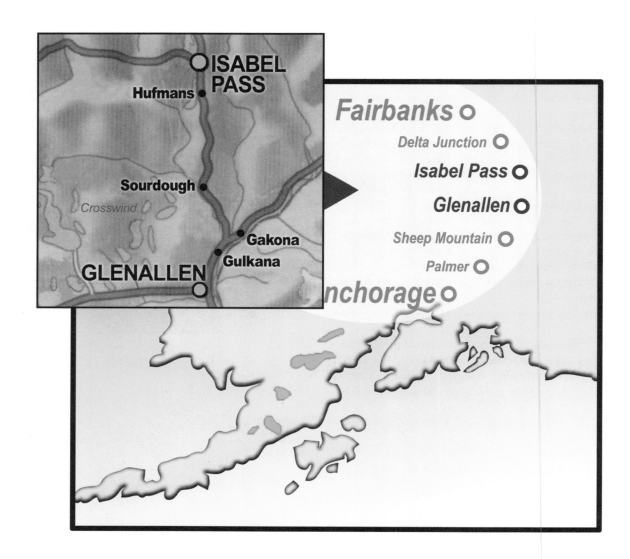

I woke up cold and wet, but the rain had stopped in the early morning. My mood was lifted when I scanned the route elevation map for Day Three. It would be a mostly downhill day as we continued south out of the Alaska Range toward the Wrangell Mountains. The declining elevation was encouraging, but the route narrative warned about several steep climbs interspersed among the downhill segments.

Our favorite campsite was Day Three where we basked in the warm Alaska sunlight late into the evening.

It was cloudy and biting cold as we packed our bags, folded our wet tents, and made token attempts to stretch out our legs and backs. As we inched out of camp, back onto the two-lane road, the sun pushed up through the overcast sky and declared that this would be a fine day.

It was, in fact, the finest day of our trip. Couched between the Alaska Range behind us, the Wrangell Mountains to our left, and the Chugach Mountains rising steadily ahead, we soaked up a wilderness wonderland. In the morning we were welcomed by Mt. Drum (over twelve thousand feet) and Mt. Sanford (over sixteen thousand feet) piercing into the blue sky. Creating their own unique weather systems, the two mountains carried cottony cloud banks on their shoulders.

The only evidence of civilization throughout the day was a periodic glimpse of the Alaska pipeline snaking its way along our same route south. Even this grandiose display of human engineering and tenacity was dwarfed by the vastness of the Alaska frontier. The pipeline was reduced to a wandering seam on the unending fabric of mountains, plains, rivers, and tundra.

The scenery energized us, and we picked up our speed across the rolling hills and along the Gulkana River. We crossed dozens of tributaries cascading down from the mountain-bound glaciers and adding to the Gulkana's broad flow. By late morning, the pack of riders had spread out more than usual, and we found ourselves alone for several miles. Without the distraction of the other riders, I relished my first clear opportunity to focus on the ride. I focused on creating perfect circles with my pedals, on maintaining deep diaphragmatic breathing, on keeping my posture straight and my upper body still, and on the passing Alaska scenery. My thoughts were bound only to my task and to the present moments. As I settled into this state of concentration, my enjoyment level rose.

Day Three started cold and wet but developed into a spectacular day.

It was not the first time that I had experienced such euphoria on my bike, and I had read of similar experiences by other riders. One professional racer named this exhilaration "the grin factor" because his intense pleasure with the riding experience would cause him to break out into an involuntary smile.* This day's stretch along the Gulkana brought to my face a broad smile that echoed my deepest pleasure with the ride. As we edged around one bend in the river and headed into a new valley, the wind picked up behind us. The tailwind shot us forward and we sailed down the valley at more than thirty miles per hour.

* Davis Phinney, "Ride Like the Wind: The Advantages of Aerodynamics," in *"Bicycling Magazine's" Complete Books of Road Cycling Skills*, ed. Ed Pavelka, p. 119.

It was like canoeing downstream in a rushing current. With only average effort, we were achieving top speeds. It was during this mystical morning that Paul started speculating about a return trip to Alaska with his family. By the end of the day, his talk had turned to buying property. Alaska had worked its alluring magic on Paul.

The lure of Alaska is a much-discussed subject. Over the centuries, different peoples' journeys to Alaska have been motivated by the promise of material treasures such as fish, furs, gold, or oil. Yet many others have been drawn by a far deeper, more emotional attraction—the opportunity to escape, to live on the sparse fringes of society, simply to be alone.

From the prehistoric wanderers who crossed the land bridge that used to connect Siberia and North America, to Chris McCandless, the twenty-five-year-old college graduate who died alone of starvation in the vast interior of the Denali National Park, people have been drawn to the open spaces where there is freedom from societal conflicts and constraints. Some, like Chris, whose tragic wanderlust was chronicled by Jon Krakauer in his book *Into the Wild,* underestimate the unforgiving nature of our harshest environments.

Chris was a philosophical disciple of people like Henry David Thoreau, who argued that life is most fulfilling when unencumbered by possessions or even by interactions with other people. In apparent pursuit of ultimate solitude, Chris hiked into the harsh Alaska wilderness with no equipment and only a small bag of rice. He survived for one hundred days before succumbing to the realities that accompany Alaska's solitude. Unlike Chris, most wilderness seekers know that being "one with nature" also means being prepared to deal with nature's often fickle behavior.

Like Paul and Bushy, Ted and I have been outdoor adventurers all our lives. The steady course of our lifelong friendship is strung together by various outdoor experiences, some more exotic than others.

Ted and I became friends sometime in the 1950s, during those early childhood years that somehow get muddled in our aging memories. The origination point

The steady course of our lifelong friendship is strung together by various outdoor experiences, some more exotic than others.

The view from our tent on the evening of Day Three.

of our friendship was the Canadian shore of Lake Erie, where both our families spent each summer. It was on this Lake Erie shore that we first developed our taste for outdoor adventure. With sleeping bags, marshmallows, and flashlights, we camped on the beach under broad starlit skies. Lulled to sleep by the water rustling over the rocks on the point, we would wake at daybreak and drag our sand-filled sleeping bags to one of our homes, where parents and breakfast awaited.

With increasing age came drivers' licenses and greatly expanded opportunities for adventure. Heading five hours north to Ontario's Algonquin Park, we undertook multi-day canoe trips, portaging between the hundreds of small pristine lakes that dot the park's interior.

While in college together, we completed our boldest adventures, making two cross-country road trips. On the first one, we squeezed nearly three thousand miles of travel into two weeks, spending time camping in the Rocky Mountains and Grand Canyon.

In the summer of 1973, on our second trip West, we did not stop in California. We hopped a charter

The Alaska pipeline.

Pamplona, Spain 1976.

flight to Hawaii, where we spent the next several weeks doing odd jobs and exploring beaches in and around Honolulu. Toward the end of our stay, we ventured to the outer islands of Maui and Kauai, where we hiked into dormant volcanoes and camped on deserted tropical beaches.

That same summer, on our return trip across the mainland, we strayed north to the Montana ranchland owned by the family of another Williams College classmate, Ed Spencer. With Ed and three others, we headed down to Wyoming for a weeklong backpack trek, mostly above tree line in the Wind River Mountains.

Three summers later, we headed the opposite direction, across the Atlantic for a wandering tour of Europe. While our budget allowed for an occasional night in a cheap hotel, we spent most nights outdoors in a variety of settings. We camped for four days in the dry moat of the Pamplona Castle among a melting pot of revelers celebrating the Spanish San Fermin Festival and the *running of the bulls*, made famous by Ernest Hemingway's book *The Sun Also Rises*. We also found solitude in camping on the deserted slope of the shoulder of Mont Blanc near Chamonix, France.

For both Ted and me, the lure of the outdoors has continued into adulthood as we and our families have made return trips to Algonquin and to new destinations in the West. In many respects, Alaska for us was much more than a biking challenge. It was a reaffirmation of our friendship and the shared outdoor experiences that helped shape that friendship over the years.

For both Ted and me, the lure of the outdoors has continued into adulthood.

27

Day Four

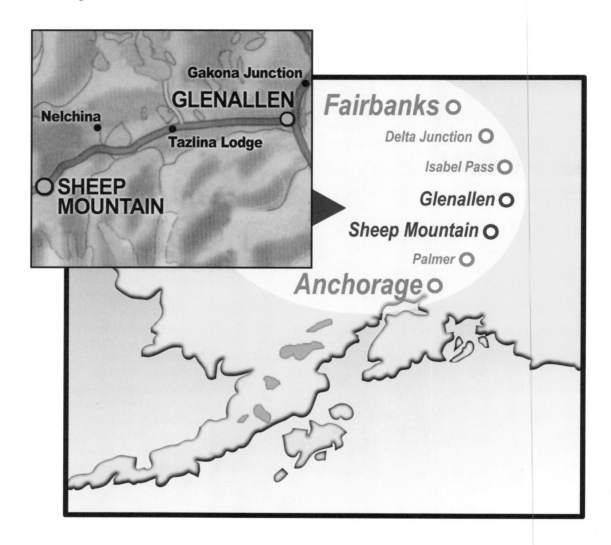

Day Four was the payback. If on Day Three we felt we had wings, on Day Four we had anchors dragging behind our bikes. The day began with an ominous twist in logistics that required us to hike two miles to where our bikes had been parked overnight. More troubling than the energy expended was the delayed start of a very challenging route.

After tracking closely to the pipeline for the last couple days, we would now part its company. While the pipeline continued south toward its terminus at the port of Valdez, our route turned more west toward the Chugach Mountains. It would be an eighty-five-mile day, nearly all uphill.

The steady, slow climb was punctuated periodically by short, severe inclines. The prevailing headwind coming out of the west threatened to push us back as we neared the top of each hillcrest. While the temperature was tolerable, the wind carried a cold drizzle that kept us in full rain gear all day.

Unlike the previous two days when we had split up, on Day Four we sensed a need to ride together. The conditions were hostile, and our camaraderie would provide moral support and security throughout the day. Riding together also meant we could employ the drafting technique we had learned in our training. Due to the inherent danger of riding so close together, drafting was forbidden by the ride organizers. We were sensitive to this policy for the first three days, but on Day Four we were in violation for most of the day. With Bushy taking the lead, we formed a single line of four bikes, each no more than three inches behind the one ahead. Bushy labored into the headwind but provided a shield for Ted, Paul, and me that helped us conserve our energy.

After five minutes, Bushy signaled his desire to drop back into the fourth spot, and each of the three other riders moved up one position. Continuing this periodic rotation, our four bikes advanced into the wind like a single smooth-running machine. On several occasions during the day, we would pick up one or two other riders who would join our lineup and enjoy the benefits of team riding for a few miles or until the next outpost. The downsides of drafting were the risk of an accident and the intense concentration required to stay just inches part. The technique also became less effective and more difficult on steep hills when we were moving laterally to pass other riders and shifting gears to deal with the incline. These sudden movements greatly increased the probability of a collision.

After our lunch stop, we faced one of the longest, steepest climbs of the week. We abandoned any attempts at drafting but remained together as we forged onward. The wet and cold crept into my core and I felt drained for the first time on the trip. I was also experiencing a biker's version of carpal tunnel syndrome, a common industrial disability that results from repetitive motions using your hands or wrists. The biker's version is caused by the extended hours spent with one's wrists bent back while gripping the handlebars. This position causes a compression of the ulnar nerve, which starts at the neck and runs through the arm and hand to the baby and ring fingers.*

Although it's possible and advisable to use different hand positions on a road bike, I was still afflicted by an increasing numbness in my left hand.

---

*"Numbness: Get Feeling Back Where It Belongs," in *"Bicycling Magazine's" Complete Books of Road Cycling Skills*, ed. Ed Pavelka, p. 169.

By the fourth day, I was unable to shift gears with my left hand, which controls the chain's movement among the three larger front chain rings, more formally known as the crankset. Ninety percent of my riding involved gear combinations that use the middle of these three chain rings. However, the smallest ring, colloquially named the "granny gear," is indispensable for climbing a long, steep hill, enabling you to keep pedaling with a fast cadence even at slow, uphill speeds. As I headed up the incline and reached the point where I needed to shift down to my granny gear for steep ascents, I would quickly reach across with my right hand to make the shift. This necessary but awkward motion often disrupted my pedaling rhythm and made hill climbing that much harder.

Leaving the final outpost on Day Four, we still had thirteen miles to reach our camp. The wind raised its strong hands, pushing back on my chest, and the raindrops grew larger. They exploded like pebbles off the plastic cover of my helmet, and I instinctively lowered my head as if I could somehow hide from the drops. I couldn't see through my rain-splattered glasses. I tucked them into my coat pocket and squinted through the wind and rain to maintain my three-foot-wide course on the roadside.

The surface conditions also deteriorated as we en-

Bushy, cold but always smiling.

countered long stretches of road construction. In preparation for repaving, the road had been scored into a choppy corrugated pattern that rattled our bikes and sent vibrations up our arms and shoulders. Even if the wind had permitted otherwise, the rough roads kept our speeds between ten and twelve miles per hour.

I checked my odometer continuously, like a schoolboy watching the classroom clock tick down the final minutes before recess. Each mile dragged on, and I recalled the comments of a friend in Buffalo who was an experienced long-distance rider: "There will be fifteen minutes of every trip that you will absolutely hate."

Before indulging in too much self-pity, I lifted my head and gazed at some of the most striking scenery in the world. The Chugach Mountains stretched out before me. Dozens of glaciers filled in the gaps that ran through the mountain ridges. The setting was a source of new energy, and I turned my thoughts away from my own discomfort and toward the pain and suffering of those who would, I hoped, benefit from this event.

From the day I signed up for the ride, I became more attuned to information and news on AIDS and the search for a vaccine. The first official report of AIDS was just twenty years ago. Here are some of the statistics:

- Twenty-two million people have died.
- Thirty-six million others are infected with the HIV virus.
- More than 70 percent (or roughly 25 million) of those infected are in sub-Saharan Africa, the poorest region in the world.
- In South Africa, 11 percent of the country's 43 million people are infected.
- Every day, about twice as many people die from AIDS as the number of those who perished in the attacks on the World Trade Center.
- The number of daily deaths would be the equivalent of twenty-four fully loaded 747s crashing every day.
- In South Africa, Botswana, and Zimbabwe, half of all fifteen-year-olds are expected to die of AIDS.
- The country of Malawi alone has over five hundred thousand orphans who have lost both their parents to AIDS.

In the United States, the disease is associated with homosexuality and intravenous drug use. This stereotype does not hold true for the rest of the world. The great majority of the worldwide victims contract the disease through heterosexual contact. The search for a cure has been greatly hindered by the virus's ability to mutate and thereby sidestep the impact of vaccines.

Expensive drug therapy has vastly improved the survival rate of those infected with the virus. While this has helped lessen the horrific effects of the disease in Americans and other victims in developed countries, this therapy is not a cure and is far too expensive for the millions of sufferers in the African subcontinent.

Dr. Peter Piot, the United Nations point person on AIDS, warns of great risks in the future. Should the disease spread to more populous regions, the current epidemic could quickly escalate to a global pandemic, affecting hundreds of millions. This is more than a theoretical risk, as India, with its one billion residents, has recently risen to the top of the list, trailing only South Africa in the number of infected citizens. Only the development of an effective vaccine can control this risk.

As I contemplated the future of my children and my children's children, the potential impact of this insidious disease became intensely personal. My newfound enlightenment revealed that this is no longer a "gay" issue. AIDS is a worldwide threat that must be addressed before it spirals completely out of control. I recognized the greater importance of my participation in this event.

Edward Abbey, a nature conservationist, once said, "Sentiment without action is the ruin of the soul." Ted, Bushy, Paul, and I were not research scientists, but as part of the AIDS Vaccine Ride, we were taking action. This thought made the last few miles of Day Four more than bearable.

"There will be fifteen minutes of every trip that you will absolutely hate."

28

Day Five

The campsite for Day Four was high at Eureka Pass near Sheep Mountain. The actual site was the remnants of a gravel pit carved out of the side of the mountain. Given the mountainous terrain, this was the only level space remotely suitable for our small army of riders. It was a tight fit as we wedged nearly a thousand tents into this sold rock enclave.

Like our other high-altitude sites, the temperature plummeted in the evening hours, and we added more layers to ward off the chill. While the campsite was harsh, it provided a spectacular vantage of the Chugach Mountains to our south. Behind us to the north, the Talkeetna rose in equal majesty.

As we surveyed our surroundings, a fellow rider pointed out some sheep meandering high above us on a steep rocky slope. I pondered what natural instincts drew these animals to such awkward and inhospitable habitations.

Following dinner, a group of native Kicaput Indians performed a traditional dance ceremony until the cold temperature chased most of us back to our tents and sleeping bags.

After our hard day of climbing into the wind and rain, we slept soundly. Although a notorious snorer, Ted had not disturbed me once on the trip. It's possible

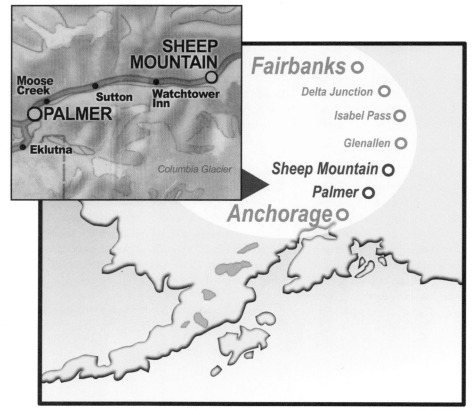

Team Ted at the end of Day Four with Sheep Mountain in the background.

that my industrial earplugs rivaled my neoprene booties for the "most valuable accessory" award on the trip.

We awoke on Day Five to a cool, gray, misty morning, with the temperature still hovering around thirty-five degrees Fahrenheit. At the food tent, we were informed that we would be bused part way down the road to Chickaloon King Mountain Lodge before retrieving our bikes for the balance of the day's journey. Having conquered the challenges of the previous day, and feeling prepared to deal with any adversity, we lobbied the Pallotta official to be exempted from the bus transport. He flatly denied our request, explaining that road con-struction made the conditions far too dangerous for bicycling. Although we reluctantly boarded the bus, we soon witnessed the wisdom of the decision. The road narrowed to a tight two-lane track carved though the northern edge of the Chugach Mountains on its way to the town of Palmer, Alaska. As we curved left and right, up and down, we came across several stretches where erosion and rockslides had reduced the road's width so severely that two vehicles could not pass. One of these constrictions appeared just past a blind hairpin turn at the bottom of a fast downhill segment. We pictured out loud the likely result of speeding around that wet curve

Breaking camp the morning of Day Five at the Eureka Pass gravel pit.

on a bicycle and having to compete for road space with a logging truck headed in the opposite direction.

Although the bus hop shortened the day's ride by a few miles, there was ample challenge ahead. Leaving the lodge, we were lulled to complacency by several long downhill rides as we continued our descent out of the Chugach range. Riding together, we hurtled on-ward, and I watched with glee the effortless miles roll up on my bike computer. As we descended to a lower altitude, the temperature warmed and we stopped to

strip off our water-resistant wind jackets. We were only twenty miles from Palmer and feeling almost lackadaisical about our easy progress. That was about to change.

The next fifteen miles were a sharp uphill ascent to the top of the pass that preceded our final exit from the mountains. This climb was the most challenging of the week. With at least a 6 percent grade, the road consisted of a series of switchbacks cut into the solid rock hillside. Its narrow two-lane width afforded no room for a shoulder, and we were forced to share the road with increasingly heavy traffic. Eighteen-wheel logging trucks roared past, leaving a wake of wind and spray. Intense awareness and communication were needed as we navigated past other riders who were pedaling slower or even walking their bikes up the inclines. We regulated our pace so that we would be free of vehicle traffic as we pulled out and around the slower riders. Maintaining such intense concentration and precision became more difficult, as the continuous climb was taxing our stamina.

The mileage indication on my computer reported that we had covered only five and half miles. That couldn't be right. I tapped the computer to make sure it was working. I started longing for a level stretch where we could stop and rest, but the road sustained its steady upward rise, moving left then right, one switchback after another. Paul was our lead rider as he often was on the climbs. He signaled back to me to be alert, and about thirty yards ahead I could see three riders off their bikes, standing in the tight strip of pavement between the rock wall and the highway. As we came closer I could see that one of them was busily trying to change a

Riding together,

we hurtled onward,

and I watched with glee

the effortless miles roll up

on my bike computer.

Ted stopping to put on his windbreaker beside one of the many glaciers flowing out of the Chugach Mountains.

Bushy led us on a spontaneous side trip to the Musk Ox farm.

flat tire while the other two were providing protection against the oncoming vehicle and bike traffic.

We had seen over fifty flat tires in the past five days, one within two miles of the start on Day One. While every outpost had a small mobile bike repair shop for mechanical repairs, all riders were forewarned that they would have to deal with their own flats. Under ordinary circumstances, changing a tire is not difficult, but trying to do so in the middle of a narrow fifteen-mile climb with the front wheel of the bike lying in the right traffic lane was another matter. Checking our mirrors to make sure we were clear of oncoming traffic, the four of us looped out and around the three stalled riders and con-

tinued our plodding ascent. I silently thanked the Almighty that Team Ted had experienced no flat tires or mechanical woes. Our luck would change within twenty-four hours.

More than ten miles to the top, the road leveled off and widened for a hundred yards before resuming its upward track. We rested and ate granola bars before restraddling our bikes for the final significant climb of the ride. The morning's complacency was gone but replaced by a pleasant sense of paradox. We were weary but felt strong. We were tired but not spent. We ached but felt fantastic. We were anxious to finish the climb but did not want it to end.

As we came out of the final switchback, we could see the crest of the hill. Following Bushy, we all stood up out of our saddles and attacked the last uphill stretch to put an exclamation point at the end of this daunting climb. We were rewarded with the sight of a final five-mile gradual descent to finish the day. As I contemplated with satisfaction the near completion of our second last day, Bushy abruptly turned right onto a side road. He had spotted a sign for an Alaskan musk ox farm, and we were all quickly convinced that it was an essential side trip.

Although the visit to the musk ox farm was less than scintillating, we were all glad we stopped. It was one of many examples of Bushy's positive influence on the trip. While I was competitively focused on the road and the miles we left behind, Bushy savored the total experience. It's not about destination; it's about the trip. There is no better metaphor for living one's life. It's a truth I often forget, and I appreciated Bushy's subtle reminders to "enjoy the ride because when you get to Anchorage, it's over."

As we glided down into Palmer, we were greeted by civilization and a crowd of local residents who cheered and thanked us for visiting their state. Our campground was a grassy field adjacent to the Palmer Fairground, where the Alaska State Fair was in full swing.

After setting camp and cleaning up, we headed over to the fair in time for the demolition derby but too late for the judging of the Spam recipe contest. There was little to distinguish this state fair from any other except the people. It was one of our few opportunities to mingle publicly with any number of local residents. I know stereotypes are dangerous, but I sensed an air of pride and simple values in these people. Behind each face was an interesting untold story. What brought them or their ancestors to this rugged environment so close to the Arctic Circle?

The sun shone until past 10 p.m. and as the dark descended, we settled by our tents with a taste of Yukon Jack to watch the fireworks. I didn't know then that the fair fireworks were only the preview. Getting up for a bathroom break at 2 a.m., I was greeted by a wondrous display of the Northern Lights dancing across the sky. It was a blazing sky theater that begged for a musical score. The North Star blazed larger and bolder than I had ever witnessed.

Standing alone in the quiet among a thousand sleeping people, I thought for a moment about rousting the other riders. But no, I decided this show was for me. As it was my last night in Alaska, I dwelled for a while in the quiet darkness, pretending I was alone.

I was greeted by a wondrous display of the Northern Lights dancing across the sky. It was a blazing sky theatre that begged for a musical score.

The Northern Lights.

29

Day Six

The *VacScene* for Day Six predicted showers for our final stretch from Palmer to Anchorage. True to Alaska's unpredictable character, we basked in seventy-degree sunshine all the way in.

Having reentered the most populous area of the state, our final day's route took us along one of Alaska's rare four-lane highways, a far less challenging track. It was on this relatively safe route that we experienced our only crash of the trip. A fellow rider, eager to get to the front of the pack, attempted to pass all four of the Team Ted riders. He passed Bushy, Ted, and me and was almost beyond Paul when he struck a rough section of the pavement and lost control. He overcompensated and slid straight sideways into Paul's front wheel. The front of Paul's bike stopped, but the back kept going and propelled him in a full somersault over the fallen rider. I veered left and Ted veered right, both of us brushing past the tangled bikes unscathed. Anyone who has witnessed an auto accident knows the unforgettable crunching sound of metal on metal. Bike accidents emit their own signature sounds that penetrate the core of all bystanders. The chaos of the crash passed, and we rushed to the sides of Paul and the other rider, both still attached to their pedals. Paul had nasty-looking patches of road rash on his thigh and elbow but was otherwise unharmed and characteristically nonchalant. In a typical case of poetic injustice, the offending rider was unscathed.

When it was apparent that there were no

injuries beyond minor "road rash," our attention turned immediately to the two bikes in the crash. Perhaps a worse fate than injury would be irreparable bike damage that would prevent either Paul or the woman from finishing the ride with only thirty miles to go on the final day. After reconnecting a chain and twisting some metal back in position, we were satisfied that both bikes would last the day.

At the outskirts of Anchorage, we turned off the highway to the safety of a paved bike path that snaked its way across gentle wooded hills. We savored this final stretch, alternately cruising together at top speed and stopping frequently to relax or to take in the sight of a pontoon plane landing on a nearby lake.

From the bike path we transitioned to the city streets of Anchorage, where we were greeted merrily by expectant residents and tourists. Many had followed our progress through reports by local television stations, and they knew the route that would take us to the city center.

With its three hundred thousand residents, Anchorage is home to nearly half of Alaska's population. The other half is sparsely distributed across the state's 590,000 square miles, a space more than twice the size of Texas and larger than the combined size of the ten smallest states in the lower forty-eight.

Located on the Cook Inlet, Anchorage is near the Matanuska Valley. This unusually fertile area was settled during the Great Depression by

Paul displaying his friendship-building skills.

impoverished farmers from the northern plains of Minnesota and the Dakotas. Facing starvation at home, these farm families accepted the federal government's offer and support to relocate in Matanuska, where "cabbages grow as large as basketballs."

Anchorage's city center is a clean, neat, treeless area just a few square blocks in area. The rising size and enthusiasm of the crowds on the sidewalk alerted us to the closeness of the finish line. Riding four abreast we made a final left turn, and almost unexpectedly the ride was over. That was it. We were done. The thrill of our accomplishment was muted by the emptiness that accompanies the end of an event that had commanded our attention and anticipation for four months.

After phone calls home and cheering the stream of riders coming in behind us, we retired to Humpty's Saloon across the street, where we toasted our feat with a Moosehead Lager.

At 4 p.m. we joined the chaos of the closing ceremonies, followed by departure logistics. Fighting through the crowds, we managed to accumulate our duffel bags and consign our bikes to a UPS agent for shipment back home. I signed the shipping form and informed the agent that there was no rush required in getting my bike back to Buffalo. But as soon as I walked away, a pang of emptiness rose up inside of me. This black-and-yellow Trek LeMond had been the focal point of my days for nearly four months. In that period, it had dutifully car-

The thrill of our accomplishment was muted by the emptiness that accompanies the end of an event that had commanded our attention and anticipation for four months.

Ted and I enjoying the final ten miles on the bike path into Anchorage.

ried my weight across twenty-five-hundred miles. I felt like a parent putting my child on the bus to go away to camp. I went back to be sure the agent had spelled my address correctly, and maybe I also gave my bike a pat on the seat as encouragement for the long trip home.

After collecting our duffel bags, we realized that we had no transportation to the airport hotel where we planned to shower and change before boarding our overnight flights back East. Volunteering to scout for a cab, I hiked to a downtown Marriott hotel a few blocks away. A woman in the lobby overheard my inquiry

about cabs, and she offered to transport the four of us and our gear in her pickup truck. Her name was Joan. She said it was on her route home, but I'm fairly sure she took us well out of her way.

Riding up front with her, I made polite conversation on the twenty-minute trip to our hotel. She had moved to Alaska by herself ten years ago. She was seeking to escape some unexplained source of unhappiness and to find a new life in this remote region. It was a familiar tale—coming to Alaska to escape and to start over. Since her arrival, she had become an avid mountain climber and was openly enamored with her new state. When I asked if she might ever move back to the lower forty-eight, she paused, turned her eyes from the road to me, and whispered an emphatic no.

As we showered, changed, and prepared for our flights home, Paul, Bushy, Ted, and I all gushed over the success of our adventure. We thanked Bushy repeatedly for initiating the idea. We shared numerous recollections that we will be sure to embellish as we repeat them in the coming years.

With the late-day sun still hanging on at 10 p.m., we boarded the shuttle bus to the airport and our return to family and work.

Postride clowning in Anchorage.

30

Homecoming

Arriving at the Anchorage Airport over an hour before our departure, Ted, Paul, and I had time to browse through the shops leading to our concourse. Bushy had left on an earlier flight. The sun was sliding beneath the horizon, somewhere out over the Bering Sea, and the final rays of the day beamed through the concourse windows.

I was hoping to buy something for Mary, Hanna, and Will. I wanted to bring them tangible evidence of my trip, more than just the verbal anecdotes that I was anxious to share. Having circled the gift shop three times, I was still not smitten by any of the shops' offerings—a coffee cup with a picture of a moose on one side and the map of Alaska on the other, various T-shirts that could just as easily have come from the Buffalo airport. I realized how impossible it was to find a souvenir that would capture our experience over the past week. With time running out, I opted for two stuffed animals—a husky for Hanna and a seal for Will—and some earrings for Mary. At least I would not be empty-handed.

Our family greeting at the Buffalo Airport.

We boarded the North-west flight headed for Minneapolis, with a change to Buffalo the next morning. It was an older plane and the seats sagged beneath us, but we still slept most of the way. After sharing some coffee and bagels with Paul in the Minneapolis airport, we parted ways with final affirmations of what a great trip it had been. Ted and I caught our flight, and two hours later, we landed in Buffalo.

Our welcoming committee was no less ardent than a family greeting a soldier son returning from the battlefront. Ginna was there with Ted's daughter, Ellie. Mary, Hanna, and Will were also there, holding a homemade "Welcome Home" sign. One of our family traditions, initiated by Mary, is to mark all important occasions with a sign. Every birthday, Hanna or Will wake up to a colorful sheet of construction paper, decorated with stars, drawings, and bold birthday greetings. The signs are one of the ways we say we care, and Hanna and Will have picked up on the tradition. The sight of the three of them holding the

Hanna and me shortly after our return.

sign and smiling as I left the plane brought forth a fresh awareness of my good fortune.

We strolled together to the baggage claim area to retrieve our bags, still marked with Alaska dirt. We headed out to our respective cars, and Ted and I stopped to say good-bye, the official end of our adventure. Hoisting his backpack on his right shoulder, he turned back to me, smiling with wide eyes, "Okay, now, where are we going to go next year?"

Epilogue

In the many months since our return, I have basked daily in a warm reflection of our Alaska ride experience. The montage of people we met, the sights we saw, the challenges we overcame, the cause we supported, and the experiences we shared still evoke an inner exhilaration for me. Lance Armstrong wrote a best seller titled *It's Not about the Bike*, a story about his victory over cancer and the new perspective it created for his life. I could have selected the same title for this narrative. The Alaska ride was about friendship, about physical and mental challenges, about supporting a critically important cause, and about adventure. But more than all, it was about life—not a passive accepting existence but the aggressive squeezing of the last drop of juice from each and every day. The ride taught us not to wait for life's offerings to appear on our doorstep. To wait is to live with anticipation and without experience. It's a pleasurable recognition that for those four months, I lived large, with risk and pain, but also with purpose and fulfillment. In the words of Theodore Roosevelt, "Far better is it to dare mighty things, to win glorious triumphs even though checkered by failure than to take rank with those poor spirits who neither enjoy much nor suffer much because they live in the gray twilight that knows neither victory nor defeat."

"Far better is it to dare mighty things, to win glorious triumphs even though checkered by failure than to take rank with those poor spirits who neither enjoy much nor suffer much because they live in the gray twilight that knows neither victory nor defeat."

Acknowledgments

Writing this account of my four-and-half-month experience preparing for and participating in the 2001 AIDS Vaccine Ride has been as enjoyable as the event itself. Finding the time to write has been at least as challenging as finding the time to train. Over four years have passed since I jotted my first notes, and I am finally pulling the last pieces together.

Many individuals warrant recognition here, mostly those who supported my efforts in preparing for and getting through the ride itself.

Ted, Bushy, and Paul, thanks for your camaraderie and for allowing me to share this experience with you.

Jim Costello, thanks for your extraordinary patience in answering my endless stream of naive questions and for making me feel welcome at Handlebars.

George Kreiner, Ted Walsh, and John Mineo, thanks for going along on those training rides.

Will Clarkson, thanks for your inspiration and joie de vie.

Mary, Hanna, Will, and my mother, Kay Gisel, thanks for your unqualified support and especially for your understanding as I disappeared for several hours nearly every Saturday and Sunday.

To my father, Bill Gisel Sr., who passed away a year before the ride, thanks for that competitive spirit, which I no doubt inherited from you.

Finally, I have had tremendous support from Faith Jantzi, who has helped me with my editing and my research. Without her, this work simply would not have come together. Thanks, Faith.